JACKY FLETCHER trained in Bristol as a teacher for children with severe learning difficulties and went on to gain the Certificate in Education, enabling her to teach in primary schools. After a short spell of working in various schools, she became a qualified swimming teacher and subsequently worked for several years in this field. While raising her family of three children, she assisted her husband with his own carpet and upholstery cleaning business, but throughout the years she has stayed connected to those with learning difficulties. She currently works as an activities co-ordinator in a large residential home for the elderly and part-time as a community support worker with adults who have learning difficulties.

She and Stefan have taken part in several TV programmes about ADHD, including *Horizon*, *UK Living* and *News at Ten* special report.

NB: All Christian names in this book have been changed.

Running to a Different Rhythm

Running to a Different Rhythm

Jacky Fletcher

ATHENA PRESS
LONDON

Running to a Different Rhythm
Copyright © Jacky Fletcher 2010

All Rights Reserved

No part of this book may be reproduced in any form
by photocopying or by any electronic or mechanical means,
including information storage or retrieval systems,
without permission in writing from both the copyright
owner and the publisher of this book.

ISBN 978 1 84748 747 6

First published 2010 by
ATHENA PRESS
Queen's House, 2 Holly Road
Twickenham TW1 4EG
United Kingdom

Printed for Athena Press

I dedicate this book to Stefan.

Contents

My Little Boy Blue	11
About ADHD	12
Preface	13
1992	17
1993	19
1994	20
1995	26
1996	28
1997	39
1998	54
1999	56
2000	79
2001	86
2002	92
2003	109
Afterword	119
Symptoms Commonly Found in Adult ADHD	121
Recommended Reading	124

My Little Boy Blue

Forget-me-not eyes – my little boy blue,
Come snuggle up close and I'll sing to you;
Your tiny body so soft and warm
As I curl my arms around your form.

I bury my face in your wonderful hair
A corn-coloured thatch beyond compare;
You gurgle contentment and wriggle with joy
My sweet little, cute little, picture-book boy.

You pad so softly about on all fours
In clockwork rhythm along the floors;
You touch and taste and look and hold –
The world is new when you're not a year old.

Your smile would lighten the darkest room,
Your chuckle would banish a heart full of gloom;
Love and warmth – laughter and joy –
It's all wrapped up in my baby boy.

About ADHD

ADHD, which stands for Attention Deficit Hyperactivity Disorder, is a very real condition, giving rise to lack of impulse control which may be due to chemical imbalances in the brain of certain neurotransmitters called dopamines. It is not an excuse for bad behaviour, as some are inclined to think. Admittedly, there are some who would 'jump on the bandwagon' and make a miscalculated diagnosis if a child, for some reason or other, displays certain characteristics of ADHD, but it is imperative that a proper medical diagnosis is undertaken. This is usually done by using the DSM-IV criteria (Diagnostic and Statistical Manual of Psychiatric Disorders), whereby the symptoms would have shown to be persistent for a period of no less than six months and would have emerged before the age of six.

Many professionals also use the patient's history in addition to problems and presenting behaviour, which can include feedback from family members, relatives and those with whom the child is associated such as teachers at school. Sometimes a computerised performance test, known as TOVA (Test of Variables of Attention), may be used. Brain scans may also be helpful.

Preface

Stefan is a much loved and much wanted son. He has two beautiful sisters. Jane is older than him by eighteen months and Louise is three years younger. All three children are very precious gifts and all equally loved, although Stefan has required much attention due to his constant struggle with ADHD, which stands for Attention Deficit Hyperactivity Disorder. The girls have, on the whole, been incredibly understanding, even though they have often missed out: for example not being able to have their friends over because they have been subjected to Stefan's highly embarrassing antics. ADHD is an extremely complicated and difficult concept to understand and deal with, and I have always maintained it would be easier if a child had a very obvious disability – like some physical disability, for instance – as people would more readily understand and not be so hasty to judge. But isn't this similar to any disorder that affects the mind, like the person suffering with depression, for example? It is far easier to understand that which is so obviously visible. Let's face it, we have all done it.

Before I had Stefan I could be very critical if I saw a child creating havoc or grossly misbehaving. I vowed that when I had children they would never, ever be allowed to misbehave in such appalling ways; that I would be the best mum ever, with impeccably raised children who would always do what they were told and always be polite and well behaved. Then we had Stefan! From then on, all my preconceptions on raising wonderfully obedient, compliant children somehow got washed right away. I found myself dealing with a small child who just did not seem to remotely understand the word 'no', and who could not in any way comply with training of any kind. The dog was easier to train!

We were perplexed, confused, irritated, upset, harassed, flummoxed, baffled, annoyed, exhausted, worried, and experienced a whole heap of other emotions which left us asking the big question: *why?* What were we doing different from any other parent which meant that this beautiful little boy of ours seemed totally impervious to any form of training or discipline? We seemed to be getting it right with the other two, so there had to be a reason. Stefan was part of a loving, caring family, with two parents who loved him very much, and surrounded by a close-knit family of relatives. We were committed Christians, praying regularly for each of our children, endeavouring to raise them according to biblical principles. We felt driven to seek a solution and so we went to our GP. We were referred to child guidance and other specialists who gave us lots of advice and strategies, which we had virtually exhausted anyway, and we were told that our son was suffering from 'hyperkinetic syndrome'. None of this was awfully helpful, and so some time later, after being driven nearly up the wall, we took him back to the GP, who eventually referred us to Great Ormond Street Hospital, where at last he received a full assessment and diagnosis.

Finally we had an answer. But it was the start of what would be a most challenging journey through his childhood and way into adulthood, drawing out the very best and worst in us as parents and presenting enormous challenges also to teachers, other parents, helpers, friends, relatives and in fact everyone with whom he associated. Other children quickly identified the differences in him and he was 'set up' on many occasions, because they found out he would do whatever they dared him to do, even if it meant lying down in the middle of the road in front of oncoming traffic. Oh yes, he would do absolutely *anything* they asked! He had little sense of danger and rushed about at high speed leaving a trail of disaster. I was horrified at first when the hospital put him on medication, and deeply saddened. I remember going home and crying. I did not want this, yet somehow deep down I knew that it was inevitable in order for him to cope with living in society.

A number of well-meaning friends and members of our family advised us to send him away to some sort of boarding school. I was quite angry that it had even been suggested. Send our son away for someone else to raise? Over my dead body! He was our son, no matter what, and no one on this earth would ever be able to love him as we did. There was absolutely no question. So we got on with the job. It stretched us at times to our very limit. It still does. But I will never give up on him. He did not ask to be born this way. He struggles every day to cope with the differences this makes to him. He is grown-up now, and still displays full symptoms of adult ADHD. He abuses substances in order to try and make himself feel more normal and to hide a lot of inner pain. Although he took himself off medication when he became an adult, he still needs it if he works, in order to help him concentrate.

In spite of everything, he is a gifted individual who displays musical and artistic abilities, is funny and extremely quick-witted, sensitive and caring towards the 'underdogs' of society; he is reckless, obstinate, irresponsible, big-hearted, generous, gregarious, highly impulsive – and has an amazing sense of humour! I have gone on to portray an insight into life with Stefan, continuing from my first book *Marching to a Different Tune*, when I charted his early years from a parent's perspective. So often books are written by 'the professionals' who seek to bring insight to the reader regarding various disabilities, which is good, and necessary; but I am writing simply as a mum, who has first-hand experience of the problems and challenges faced when living with a child or young person with ADHD.

I have continued here to chart his life throughout his teen years and into early adulthood in the form of a diary, similar to my first book, *Marching to a Different Tune*. I have also included a few instances from his earlier years that were in that book. I hope that it will bring you, the reader, to a greater knowledge and understanding of the nature of this highly complicated, misunderstood and often misdiagnosed disorder, which has often been dismissed as just being 'very naughty'. Oh yes, he could be just plain naughty, just like any other child on this earth. Not every single act on his part could be put down to ADHD – we were acutely aware of this fact. No, I am talking about the thousands of instances where he put his own life at risk, where that 'filter' seemed to be missing regarding response to situations. Also, we did not want him to use the term ADHD as an excuse or a cop-out, so we attempted to be careful not to let him become a 'victim'.

Having said that, in all honesty there were times as he grew older when he did precisely that, being manipulative or blaming everything on his ADHD. We did not always get it right. We were too hard on him. Then at other times we were too soft. We were driven to mental exhaustion over and over again. All I can say, in retrospect, is that as a mother of a child with extremely challenging behaviour, I did my best. My very, very best.

Stefan at two years

1992

21 FEBRUARY

It was half-term. Today it was Stefan's birthday! I took him and three friends plus my two daughters to an indoor adventure place. It was buzzing with children and activities. Stefan pushed a little girl hard down a slide, upsetting her. He slapped another little girl's face. He swore at a mother. How embarrassed and ashamed I felt! The next day we made a trip to a local beauty spot where there are some beautiful lakes. Stefan chucked a stone, hitting a little girl's fingers. He began to cause friction among other children who were climbing trees and playing happily.

Just at the end of the half-term holiday, one evening, he found a tin of emulsion paint in the garage and opened it, thinking he would paint the woodwork in his room. Somehow he managed to tread it all over the garage and into the house, and covered his clothes with it. Apart from these few 'minor' little incidents it was a fairly peaceful half-term.

March

Stefan woke up really 'high' today. He remained 'high' all day at school. He was disruptive during assembly at his school and running around the school corridors. He often steals things from the cupboards at home and I have to hide a lot of things. A couple of the children's friends came to tea. He threw a lot of earth onto the patio. I gave him a broom and made him clear it up. He pushed one of the smaller children over, so I sent him to his bedroom to calm down for ten minutes. At teatime, he rubbed the strawberry jelly I had made for the children all over his hands, so he got sent to his room again. He constantly ran out into the front garden after being warned not to because of the traffic.

November

I was saying prayers with Stefan just before settling him for the night. I prayed first. 'Sorry, God, that I snapped today when things got too much.' Afterwards Stefan wanted to examine my neck. I asked him what he was doing. 'I want to see the place where you snapped,' he innocently replied.

Stefan and his sisters

1993

21 FEBRUARY

It was half-term again. Stefan's birthday usually falls during half-term. He was eight. He had a sleepover with three friends. He became wildly excited and rushed all over the house making loud noises, shrieking and shouting. He does not seem to hit other children quite so much as he used to, although he is still somewhat unpredictable. He will shove his younger sister Louise around or fight with other boys, sometimes becoming rather too aggressive. He needs little sleep compared to other children and has enormous stamina. Half-term was rather enjoyable. I took the children to see a film called *Honey, I Blew up the Kids*. He will sit through a film now, if he is interested in it. He made some things in the garage with a hammer and nails, although he opened a tin of paint again and got it all over other things. It must be something to do with having a birthday! He loves riding his mountain bike, and he started a boys' football training session on the Saturday. (Unfortunately this did not last long as his lack of social skills let him down.) He still shows off in front of other children and people a great deal, sometimes quite badly, shouting or jumping around and drawing attention to himself. When he goes to people's houses he usually comes back with something he has 'found' there – a coin, a medal or some jewellery. He has a magpie instinct to take things – especially things that glitter! I have had to stop his visits to one friend on a temporary basis to let him know that he cannot pinch things that are not his. He vehemently claims he 'finds' them!

1994

January

Stefan wanted crisps after the Boys' Brigade meeting. I said, 'Not this time,' as he had had crisps in his lunchbox that day. I also said that if he tried it on with his dad (who was collecting him, and whom I would not be able to see beforehand to warn!), he would not get away with it. When he arrived home from Boys' Brigade, Vaughan said, 'Stefan bought two packets of crisps – one for him and one for me.' I asked him where he got the money from, as I had only given him enough for his subs.

'Stefan told me he had taken extra money for them,' said Vaughan. (Found out later that it had been pinched from Vaughan's drawer!) So despite what I had said earlier, he went off knowing full well his plan of action and had defied me yet again. I told him 'no supper' and that he would not be allowed to take his friend for the weekend on holiday with me. It probably seemed I was making a mountain out of a molehill over something comparatively trivial, but I am trying to work on the principle of not allowing him to disobey clear instructions and to understand that there are consequences to his actions. The consequences have to be strong enough to make him think, although as yet nothing seems to work. It is terribly frustrating. Always I am trying to think up some deterrent which will get to him enough, but it does not seem to make any difference. There seems to be no way of stopping Stefan from doing what he is bent on doing. Punishments, deprivation of things and reasoning have little effect.

Stefan was very wakeful at night, as usual, on the medication he has been prescribed for his ADHD. I let him stay up until a quarter past nine for a special treat. I then settled him in bed, with kisses and cuddles. I also told him strictly, 'No getting out of bed!' I made sure he was comfortable and had been to the toilet, etc.

There was no reason to get out of bed. I told him that if he disobeyed he would be in trouble. I got him to repeat this back to me so that he understood what I was saying. He appeared tired and feigned extreme exhaustion.

After being downstairs for just ten minutes, I heard him moving about upstairs. I went up quickly and caught him just getting into bed with a bag of biscuits. I reprimanded him severely as he tried to make excuses. I told him he was not to get out of bed again or he would have a smack, and went back downstairs. Not ten minutes later he was out of bed again. He got one smack. He cried and told me he hated me. I reminded him that he had been warned and had made his choice. Finally he went to sleep unhappy. I too felt extremely unhappy and upset. Why does this child persist in disobedience, knowing he will get punished? It is as though he prefers the punishment and thinks in reality he will not get one. But he does get various punishments carried out if he disobeys us.

March

Vaughan and I were trying to have a bit of a lie-in on a Saturday, when we heard a lot of laughter. Vaughan jumped out of bed and looked out of our bedroom window. Louise and Stefan were dancing naked on the front lawn. Shock horror! He ran downstairs and dragged them in, reprimanding them and sending them to their rooms. Meanwhile he discovered that Stefan had tipped the chair in the lounge upside down and had cut open the underneath lining to look for 'things'. In doing this he had also broken both of the arms of the chair. Later on in the day, he climbed onto the roof when Vaughan was up there painting. After being told to go back inside he threw his cycle ramp out of Louise's bedroom window onto next door's garden. Another time he decided to use the hose… *inside* the garage. I made him clear up the mess himself.

Despite being on his medication, Stefan is still very 'high'. A babysitter came in one evening to give Vaughan and me a much-needed break for a few hours. She found Stefan in the kitchen poking a stick down the toaster, which he had switched on. He was later found lighting candles. The next morning he filled up his mouth with most of a packet of baby wipes and pulled them out of his mouth one by one. Later that evening he took an egg out of the fridge and mixed it with loads of talcum powder, making his own special concoction.

April

Stefan smashed our patio glass door with a stick. (Accidentally – I *think* – but who knows!)

During another lovely sunny afternoon, Stefan was playing happily in the garden with Louise. I checked on them several times. They were making a den. All seemed normal and peaceful for once. Vaughan was dozing in the lounge. A sudden rapping on the window woke him up while I was upstairs seeing to my oldest daughter, Jane, who was not well. It was our next door neighbour. Apparently Stefan had managed to get a huge Formica worktop out of Louise's window onto the flat roof just below and it was now overhanging the roof like a see-saw. It could have tilted over at any time and fallen on top of the people in the next garden below.

Our long-suffering babysitter came to the house for a couple of hours one evening. At bedtime Stefan managed to tip the contents of the medicine cabinet out. He was apparently 'making a mixture'. He had mixed a new bottle of Calpol with half a bottle of Dettol, Ventolin syrup, Vic and nasal drops, among other things. Also he had pinched loads of my cakes out of my freezer. Stefan uses up so much of my stuff, breaks things and smashes things, causing so much damage and costing us such a lot of money to replace things…

The following day when we were out shopping Stefan walked across the road straight in front of a car. How it missed him I shall never know! A few days previously Vaughan made a campfire with the children. Knowing his attraction to fires, Stefan was warned never to try to make a fire himself. Needless to say, when I went into his bedroom later that day he had made one with firelighters and had just lit it. I hastily extinguished it. It does not bear thinking about what could have happened if I had not gone in at that point. He needs constant monitoring!

May

Stefan went to play at a friend's house as the mother was willing to have him, to give me a little respite. He tipped a whole bucket of water over himself while fully clothed. The following week he went again. This time he got a bit bored with their dartboard and so threw darts at their new settee. The mother terminated the visits.

One day I had all the three children in my car along with Louise's friend, whom I was going to drop home after school. Stefan sat in the front seat. I got out of the car very quickly to deposit the child back to her house. I was only a minute but, even in that brief moment, Stefan let off the handbrake. I turned round to see the car rolling backwards down the hill. I sprinted to the car, yanked open the door and slammed the handbrake on, saying a few terms of endearment (not!) to my son. If I had not acted so quickly, I cannot bear to think what the outcome may have been. I think that my reactions have become razor sharp since we have had Stefan, as he is so quick to act on his impulsive thoughts, although he has usually done the deed before I find out. I only hope I don't slow down for a number of years yet!

June

Stefan put two pinball games of his in the middle of our road and watched with glee as the unwitting cars rode over them, smashing them to smithereens all over the road.

During a weekend in Kent at my sister and brother-in-law's holiday chalet, Stefan spent much time swimming in the indoor pool. Then I found out that he had taken stones from the sauna room and thrown them into the pool, along with planks of wood. The manager went mad. I had to go and explain about Stefan and make peace with him. He was not a happy man. When we left the site to return home I am sure he breathed a sigh of relief.

I took the children to our local park for a picnic. Jane had taken her shoes and socks off on the grass to run around. I glanced over to the small pond nearby to see that Stefan had floated her nice leather shoes, still with the socks inside, on the water. He then went and annoyed some older boys. They appeared to be getting quite angry towards him. It was starting to look nasty. Time to pack up and leave!

One evening, I really wanted to watch a particular programme on TV, so I decided to leave Stefan unattended with the other two children for once, in the other room. What a mad fool I must have been! First of all he decided to make his dad a cup of tea as it was Father's Day. He climbed up to the cupboard and got out my best bone china set, chipping a plate. After this he went up into his bedroom and tipped a whole tin of talcum powder over his carpet and out of the window onto the patio, and all over his younger sister. Not satisfied with these misdemeanours, he then got a jar of Marmite from the cupboard, stuck his fingers in it and smeared it all down the back of Jane's T-shirt (which she was wearing), and then smeared the rest over Louise's arm.

July

We were round at a friend's house. Stefan found some tadpoles in their pond. He managed to extract them with a net and placed them in the children's paddling pool.

When Stefan came out of school one day soon after this, he told me that there had been great excitement at the school that day. About twenty or so boys had watched a helicopter flying quite low so they had all decided to try and attract its attention for a bit of a laugh. They waved their arms and their pullovers in the air and the helicopter flew low to see what the trouble was. The pilot had waved his finger at them and they had all got into trouble. Later on in the day, Stefan said that the story was not true. What a vivid imagination he has!

November

Stefan wiped peanut butter all over Jane's brand new dress. He got into his wardrobe and weed all over his carpet.

Big cuddles

1995

Probably one of the worst New Year's Eves ever! The children were given a dog for Christmas. The cat weed in the bathroom because it was too scared to go downstairs and face the new dog, Pepsi. Jane accidentally knocked a whole bowl of slushy cat food from the landing right down the stairs, spilling it everywhere. A series of other mishaps rendered me unable to view things dispassionately and my husband had spent all day, every day, for the past week out of the house on a flat-cleaning process, not getting home until mid-evening. By the time he got back this particular night I was in an unfit state to be called a mother! The kids had argued incessantly and I had ended up shouting. Vaughan suggested I went out for half an hour to cool down, which I did. I sat in our local park and spent some time praying before making an impromptu visit to my sister's house nearby.

I then returned home, feeling a little better, and my sister and her husband popped down at eleven thirty to see the New Year in with us all. Stefan was in a highly excitable state and threw peanuts all over the lounge carpet while I struggled to maintain decorum. I think my sister and husband picked up the strained atmosphere of us trying to be happy and not making a very good job of it, and disappeared soon after the New Year was welcomed in. Poor things! I bet they wished they had not come.

We were advised by the specialist at the hospital to give Stefan a 'drugs break' sometime during school holidays and let him go without his medication for a short period of time. On the commencement of the new term, we resumed his tablets. What an angel he was that first day back on them! What a transformation! Pity it was not to last. One Sunday some of the other children in the Sunday school started to call Stefan 'mental'. He immediately retaliated in typical 'Stefan style' – aggressively. We were told that from now on we would have to pick him up early from Sunday school. That squashed any chance we had to catch up with friends for a quick chat immediately after our service had finished, while we had a few moments to ourselves.

1996

January

Every single day we have things to contend with. Broken glass, jars, bottles, ornaments smashed or hacked to bits, leaving trails of glass or china or pottery all over the floor. Then there is the constant hitting of Stefan's young sister by him. Or taking tins of food from the cupboard and opening them in his bedroom, going into the freezer and taking huge scoops of ice cream, or dipping his fingers into desserts or cakes made for occasions, leaving indentations. Or throwing himself around the lounge, leaving mess strewn around, not to mention his bedroom, which is in a terrible clutter and where I lose a constant battle trying to maintain some sort of order.

It becomes a never-ending wear and tear on our time, emotions and energy. If I give Stefan three instructions such as, 'Go upstairs, get your clothes on, and pick up your pyjamas,' he is unable to respond to all three and may begin to do one thing, only to become distracted and end up somewhere else doing something completely different. This, I learned, was one of the very typical behaviours displayed by ADHD children. We learned that only one instruction should be given at a time and the parent needs to follow it through by ensuring it is carried out, if necessary by taking the child and using clear concise phrases to encourage completion of the one task before moving on to the next. Vaughan found this much more difficult than me, as he thought Stefan should 'learn to listen'. I think that after many times of trying his own tactics he came to realise that Stefan was not just 'being naughty', but that he really did only hear the first thing.

February

I decided to try and keep a record of the consequences of Stefan's behaviour at school, at home and outside the home in an attempt to build a more consistent structure, as advised by the consultant at Great Ormond Street Hospital. Stefan had been attending on a monthly basis for some years now, and there he had been diagnosed with ADHD (Attention Deficit Hyperactivity Disorder) and he receives medication which is carefully monitored. In order to educate myself about this disorder, I started to attend conferences that were periodically held in London and other cities and tried to learn as much as possible about how to cope and deal with the enormous challenges that his behaviour presented, and then to help other people associated with Stefan to better understand. We also joined up with a national support group.

So often we are severely criticised for having an 'unruly' child, and we have lost many friends as a result – people who do not invite us to their homes for fear of what Stefan may do. I cannot say I blame them somehow. I would probably be the same if I did not have such a child. Who knows? Anyway, today we were told that he had spat all over a child at school. He had been severely reprimanded by his teacher and by his dad too, when he got home. He had also run from the class before the bell had rung, resulting in another ticking off.

A little boy knocked on our door one afternoon and came in to play with Stefan. Stefan had some very realistic toy handcuffs which he decided to use on this poor little chap, handcuffing him to his bed. He then told us he had 'lost' the key. The child became very distressed while we searched everywhere and eventually found the key. Then we released the poor child, who had been there some time by now, and sent him home. His mother appeared on our doorstep later on that evening. We had some explaining to do. Stefan has a fascination with handcuffs, knives, matches and guns – in fact everything and anything that speaks of danger or excitement.

I had bought a nice box of biscuits as a gift for one of my friends. Usually I have to hide anything that I do not want taken away in a locked box, but this time the box was full and I had nowhere to hide the biscuits. Of course, the dear boy found them, opened them and sneaked some out. The next morning, instead of going mad at him, I tried a different tactic. I told him that I was very sad he had spoilt my friend's present. In usual glib fashion he promised to buy some more. He may have had the intention of doing so in his mind at the time but of course he did not replace them. Vaughan told him he would have to forego his pocket money for a couple of weeks.

On a Sunday I cook a roast dinner followed by quite a filling dessert, like apple pie or a fruit crumble. Stefan had eaten a large dinner, and it was not long before bedtime as we had decided to eat late this particular day. He then declared that he was hungry. This is a habit he has got into and that we are trying to break, as he could not possibly have been hungry after the huge amount he had eaten. We said that he could not have any more food and he became very angry. Somehow he managed to break open my locked box and pinched all the sweet things from it and ate them in bed. When I questioned him later, he totally denied it. As a consequence I took his money to pay for the things he had eaten. He was very annoyed with me and told me I had no right to. I calmly explained that I had as much right as he had to break into my box.

March

Stefan is a good swimmer, flashing through the water like a little fish. He has been properly trained (on a one-to-one basis, of course) and now is able to go to early morning training with the other children in the club. There was an upset one particular morning. Stefan sneaked a penknife from somewhere into his swimming bag and took it out in the boys' changing rooms, where naturally I am not allowed to venture. It caused quite a rumpus among the boys. One of the dads, who cannot stand Stefan (or me, because I am his mum, I suppose), was extremely reactive and aggressive and I got rather upset by the whole business and ended up running out of the club. The chairman of the club rang me that night and said that they would have to suspend Stefan until the following week after they had held a 'committee' meeting about him.

4 MARCH

Stefan filled an old sock with paper and sprayed deodorant all over it. He hoped to set it alight. He told me it was his 'bomb'. Last evening his dad had been showing him how to light matches. I was quite nonplussed.

6 MARCH

At school today, the teacher moved Stefan to another desk for her own convenience, not as any punishment for Stefan. He hated the change. He tore all his project work up. He was sent to the head teacher, who made him sit on a chair outside the office for five hours. During this time he asked to go to the toilet and shook a little boy who happened to be in there. The head teacher was extremely frustrated to learn of this. On analysis I knew that Stefan found change difficult to handle, which is why he had torn up his work. To be made to sit for such an extreme length of time was downright cruel, especially considering the fact they were dealing with a hyperactive child who at the best of times found it difficult to sit still. I felt terribly sorry for him but I also knew that the school was struggling to contain him and was going to make mistakes. On the whole they managed to contain him well, providing him with extra assistance, and like us, they were still learning about the condition and were going to get it wrong sometimes.

We had made a decision to try and teach Stefan the value of money by giving him a monthly allowance and helping him to understand he had to use a bit at a time and not all in one go. He used up the allowance almost immediately and then stole some of his sister's money from her savings box. She was very upset as she had been saving up for her holiday. He went out and bought chocolate bars and biscuits from the local shop to 'make a pudding'. Stefan denied that he had taken his sister's money, but eventually, after prolonged questioning, he confessed. I reinforced the wrongness of taking other people's things and told him that he would have to repay the money either by earning it or selling something of his.

7 MARCH

I feel miserable today. And lonely. I am trying to cope with so many issues with the children and my family, including the temporary suspension of Stefan from the swimming club. I feel betrayed, let down, forsaken. Anyway, God knows everything. So I will continue to trust Him.

8 MARCH

I was so encouraged to learn that Stefan had paid back the money he took from his older sister. He had sold some attractive pens to his younger sister. It transpired he had been selling his older sister's pens to her! I think this is what is meant by 'robbing Peter to pay Paul', as the saying goes! I made him give the pens back. We are back to the original plan of him earning some money to repay her properly.

The chairman of the swimming club rang today and told me the outcome of the committee meeting with the parents. They have decided to suspend Stefan permanently. I was so shocked that I could hardly speak to him. What drastic action! The child of the man who dislikes Stefan so much, and who had apparently thrown Stefan's bag across the changing room, causing the penknife to fall out of it, got off scot-free! Stefan will be absolutely devastated when I have to tell him that he cannot swim with the club any more. He was getting on so well. I was later told that the two teachers who had him for lessons and training were angry at the decision but were overridden. They liked Stefan, and once they had learned how he ticked, managed to get some successful sessions with him.

I told Stefan the following day. As anticipated, he was devastated. I made a decision to withdraw Louise as well. She had not been going for long to the club, and I could not face walking in and seeing all those parents there who had voted Stefan out. I signed them both up with another swimming club in Southend. They were happy to take on the challenge of Stefan, even after I had spoken to them about the various behaviours he was likely to display. I asked them not to take him on if they felt they would not be able to cope, as it would be more damaging to let him start, get him involved and then change their minds. After a week or so of trying him out and experiencing at first hand some of the antics he got up to, they assured me that they would allocate someone to be with him every week to keep a watchful eye on him, and that they would certainly not drop him. I felt so thankful. I always remained in the spectators' area during his swimming sessions so that I was on hand in case anything untoward happened.

Stefan was like a little fish in water

It was open day at school. Stefan tore up all his Maths and English books and put them in the bin along with all his reward sticker charts. He also split open some ink cartridges and dribbled them out of his mouth and wiped the ink all over his hands. His teacher told us he had had a very bad day today. The school has tried to clamp down hard on him in order to prepare him for senior school, but it seems the harder he is clamped on, the worse his behaviour becomes.

Stefan has the best bedroom in the house. It is a large room that is completely pine clad. Tonight he decided to strip some of the panels of pine from his walls. His dad went ballistic!

One morning during late March, Vaughan and I were lying peacefully in bed when, *crash!* It sounded as though a door had fallen down. We weren't far wrong. Then we heard Stefan's plaintive voice. 'Dad, Dad, I'm hurt. Come quickly!'

Vaughan rushed out of bed and into the bathroom. Stefan was leaning over the bathroom basin with blood pouring from his face. At the sight of the mess his face was in, and being the brilliant first-aider that I am, I started to feel all 'swimmy'. Vaughan mopped up some of the blood to reveal a huge deep gash stretching from the side of his nose to just above his lip. Another gaping wound was at his temple, with one nostril badly cut. He told us he had fallen through the plate glass door in the lounge.

Shortly he began to feel the effects of the shock and turned mighty pale. I got dressed quickly and put him in the car and set off hastily to the casualty department at hospital. After a half-hour wait we were taken into a sort of operating room which housed a large bed, big lights and all sorts of other equipment. After another few moments the surgeon entered. He explained that he was a facial specialist. He had to administer two local anaesthetic injections, one in Stefan's gum and one in the side of his face where the second injury was. The poor child – he did suffer, as it was very painful. He threatened to inject the surgeon in the backside!

After some time, Vaughan arrived to take over while I drove the girls to their riding lesson. Vaughan and Stefan were home an hour or so later. Stefan's face had been neatly sewn up but it still looked a mess. He may have some remaining scars for life. He had to have the stitches removed a couple of weeks later. The rest of the day he was his usual active self. Meanwhile, our lounge door had to be completely stripped of glass, which Vaughan did before going off to golf for the rest of the day. There was glass everywhere.

28 MARCH

Stefan has had two awful days at school. He kicked one child and pushed another down some steps. He covered his hands with black ink, doing very little schoolwork, and generally being a nuisance. I wonder if the antibiotics he is taking for his facial injury do not mix well with his tablets. He has been keeping an old shoe tied to his desk which is his 'pet dog'. Every afternoon before he leaves school he puts it to bed in his desk.

April

Stefan went out for the day to some organised activities in our local country park. This was a rare occasion. I love him so very much but it was a nice break. Things were normal for a day. Well, not quite a day. He brought back a little friend to play after the country park activities were over. They were playing in the garden when all of a sudden he tipped a bucket of water all over the child, drenching him from head to foot.

30 APRIL

Vaughan and Stefan seemed to clash all day. Finally I caught a glimpse of Stefan rushing up the stairs with Vaughan in hot pursuit, eyes glaring and shouting at him to get in his bedroom. I wondered what on earth this episode was all about. On questioning, Vaughan retorted, 'I don't believe it! He's now *abseiling* down the side of the house!' I turned away to hide a smile, suddenly seeing the funny side of it. I mean, if I did not have any sense of humour, do you not think I would be in a mental asylum by now? Apparently he had tied one end of a rope to his sister's bed and hung the other end out of the window and was going down the wall.

May

Stefan has been showing aggressive behaviour at school. He punched a boy in the mouth and made it bleed. He kicked several other children.

I am so fed up with Stefan pinching things out of my cupboards, including food and money, that today I bought a thick wire rope and padlock and locked up all my money and things from my food cupboard that I did not want taken. Stefan spent the following days bending wire coat hangers and sliding them through the locked cupboard doors in an attempt to get hold of the 'forbidden fruit'...

His latest obsession is that he wants a budgie! He goes on about it day and night. He managed to get hold of an old hamster cage from a neighbour and made a cut-out model of a bird and put it in the cage. Constantly he talks about it, asking the cost of a proper cage, bird food and so on. Once he gets an idea into his head he does not easily give it up.

June

The swimming club dropped Stefan after just three months. So much for their promises to keep him! I felt hurt, upset and angry that this had happened, especially as I had gone to some lengths to explain how he was and had asked them not to enlist him in the club if they did not think they would manage to contain him. They had given him a trial period and had assigned one-to-one assistance during the lessons. I often wonder what long-term effects this could have on him, receiving rejection after rejection. Already he has very low self-esteem and once told me that he was made of 'rubbish'.

A few days later Stefan picked a fight with two boys, taunting them and calling them names. Is it, I wonder, because he feels so bad about himself that he tries to bring others down? Later on in the week his carer came in to look after him. We had waited eighteen months for respite care and when it was finally granted, it was only ninety minutes, just enough time to nip up to the local supermarket and get the week's shopping done in peace. I was grateful even for that short spell of time. While I was gone, Stefan climbed up into our loft. He found a large suitcase packed full of old photos, some in glass frames. He wanted them down. In true Stefan style, he just dropped the whole caseful out of the hatch and onto the landing. Every single photo frame was smashed. I think the carer needs respite! Also during this week he set fire to a bin in the local park. He is totally fascinated by fire – very worrying.

July

Today I watched as Stefan threw lots of different items over the fence into next door's garden, and then said to the dog in a voice loud enough for the neighbours to hear, 'Pepsi, you mustn't do that!'

Stefan stood at the end of our driveway with a concertina, our dog on a lead and a box by his side, asking passers-by for money for Great Ormond Street Hospital. He collected a few pounds. The next day he went to his friend's house and did the same thing on his driveway and collected £10. He realised he was on to a good thing, and that same evening he decided to visit another friend down the road and enlist his help. They went up and down our road, knocking on doors and saying that they were collecting for Great Ormond Street. I did not hear about this until a little later when the report came back to me that they had been saying to people, 'Hello, we are collecting for Great Ormond Street. We are hyperactive and we are patients there. Please give some money.'

His friend actually does attend the hospital, like Stefan, so at least they were telling the truth. Stefan tried to keep the money but I explained that it was dishonest to do so, especially after saying what they were collecting for. I made him hand it over and we wrote a letter together enclosing a cheque for the amount and we sent it off to the hospital. I also banned him from doing any more collecting and explained that it was not safe for him and his friend to go knocking on doors together.

Stefan is an extremely alert child. His eyes do not miss much. He has always been like this since he was a tiny baby. He could sense when I had gone out of the room from just three weeks old and would start to cry. He can recall events, descriptions and details that many of us would miss. Sometimes it can be most useful. Like the time he was outside the swimming pool playing with about a dozen other children. He was the only one who noticed a thief sidle up to a bicycle padlocked to a post and surreptitiously sever the chain using some sort of tool and ride off on the bike. Stefan alerted me and I rang the police. They arrived within five minutes and took a statement from him. He was able to fill them in with details. He was our little hero that day. Later on during the week he was included in the Borough Schools swimming gala. He won a silver medal. He also won a certificate of merit for coming first in the boys' relay. We were certainly the proud parents that week! What a change!

But, oh dear! Did he make up for it the following week! He forgot to take his tablet one day. He caused absolute chaos at school, climbing on the units and jumping on things. He went wild! A few days later at school he picked up a child over his shoulder and dropped him, bumping his head quite badly.

August

I know it sounds crazy but I actually enjoy the summer holidays with the children home from school, even though I am forever having to keep a watchful eye on Stefan. I love to organise outings and little treats for them all, or take a picnic on the beach. This summer we spent many days there and I bought a rubber boat which kept Stefan happy for many hours while I watched him rowing along the shore. There were intermittent clashes with other children, with some stone throwing and mud-slinging, but on the whole he was quite good. The two girls always love the water, and all being good swimmers I can keep a vigilant eye on them but relax as well.

1997

April

Stefan has an obsession for a little girl at the senior school that he attends, as he has turned twelve. He talks about her all the time. There was an incident at the school today during the last lesson. Stefan was accused of touching the little girl's breast. I got called in by the head of year. Stefan denied it. The following day I decided to ring the child's home to try and get things sorted out. The mum said that her daughter had indeed accused Stefan of this. I felt terribly upset and depressed by this information. My stomach was in knots. I spent a lot of time crying secretly. For two days following this incident, Stefan was kept in isolation at school. On the third day I was informed he was to be suspended for a further few days. Meanwhile the child's mother had been to the police. I thought this was a complete overreaction. Stefan was then subjected to a police interrogation about the incident, which frightened him.[*]

The very day he returned to school, a lady accused Stefan and his two friends walking home together of putting a traffic cone in the middle of the road in the line of oncoming traffic. She reported them all to one of the staff members, who chased them in his car and told them to report to the head teacher the next day. I spoke to each boy in turn. They all said that another boy on a bike had moved the cone into the road. The head teacher gave Stefan a detention nevertheless. I sometimes think that it is a case of 'give a dog a bad name'…

May

---

[*] As an adult in his twenties now, Stefan remembers this frightening incident and is adamant that the girl's accusation was false.

Stefan has a new obsession: kites! He sent off for a mail order one that he had seen in a magazine. It arrived today. After school I took him to fly it at a local beauty spot near an old castle ruins, high up on a hill. During the next few days we made repeated visits in order for him to have more fun with it. Each day, the same request was asked: 'Can you take me to fly my kite?' Anything to keep him out of trouble. One afternoon, after I had taken him, he insisted on returning later in the evening for another kite-flying session with his dad.

13 MAY

Kites!

14 MAY

Kites!

15 MAY

The obsession continues. He begged a large kite from our neighbour. He even tries to make them. With his home-made efforts he runs around outside, trying desperately to get them to fly, without much success. Most days he asks to be taken to one of his favourite haunts in his lunchtime or after school, whatever the weather. I have stood in the blasts of cold air or in the rain holding one end of a kite while he launches it for the umpteenth time.

I am also trying to stop him constantly taking stuff into school that the teachers do not want. Today he smuggled a small container in under his jacket. It was full of tadpoles!

Somehow he managed to find another tadpole the following day and take that one into school.

Stefan told a teacher one day, 'You've got big boobs.' He was isolated as a result the next day and then suspended the following day.

He decided to climb one of our tallest conifer trees in the back garden. He became completely stuck. Conifer trees become quite flimsy towards the topmost branches. How he managed to perch himself up there, I shall never know. Our neighbour brought in his ladder to attempt to retrieve him. The tree would not bear his weight. We were at a loss as to what to do and Stefan was getting panicky and just could not get down. In the end we had to call the fire brigade, who eventually managed to rig up a very tall free-standing ladder near to the top of the tree and carry him down safely. How embarrassed I felt, even though they were so kind about the whole thing!

A couple of days later we were at the swimming pool. Some children wound Stefan up by calling him names, so he clouted a boy over the head with a book. The mother complained.

Stefan came with me one day to visit an elderly gentleman from our church who had shingles and was not at all well. On the way home he asked, 'Has Uncle S got rabies?'

That evening he had a friend to stay for the night. He does not cope well with different or exciting situations. He was awake and very lively until after midnight. At five thirty in the morning he was awake again, jumping around, chatting loudly and full of life. We have a large dog flap built into our back door in the kitchen. He kicked it so hard that the whole thing shattered. Now we had a gaping hole in the back door. Inevitably he soon discovered it was much more fun to go in and out through the hole than use the door handle.

Stefan went out to the beach by himself during that weekend. He went out in the mud too far and got stuck in a moored boat on an incoming tide. Fortunately for him he was spotted by the coastguard, who called a rescue boat to fetch him in. It got into the local papers! Front page!

At the end of May, Vaughan told me he wanted to change our car. He said, 'I don't want Stefan to bite the headrests off.' *What?*

June

Whoopee! We're off to Miami! The first surprise was that Freddie Laker himself was on our plane! So we knew we were off to a good start. During the flight of nine hours, Stefan somehow managed to 'collar' the top man himself without us knowing and inform him that it was our wedding anniversary. Sir Freddie appeared at our side with a bottle of champagne and sat and had a drink with us. Neither of us had the heart to tell him that our little blighter had exaggerated the date by a fortnight! Needless to say, it was an excellent flight with two enjoyable in-flight meals, individual video TVs to watch, with music and headphones provided. The drinks were all free and the wine got to me a bit, but I just could not say no! Stefan was up and down from his seat throughout the entire flight, hardly staying put long enough to eat his meal, chatting up all the air hostesses and giving them all hugs. This made Vaughan very uptight. The plane could not land for over an hour due to storms and a tornado around Miami. We circled in a hundred-mile radius several times before finally managing to land. We later learned that June is the stormy month.

We picked up a hired car and had to pay extra airport taxes and insurances before we left the airport. It was quite hairy driving in the dark, on the wrong side of the road and not really knowing where we were going. I drove, with everyone encouraging me. We managed to find a hotel near to the apartment we had previously booked through a friend, as we could not get in it until the following day. Stefan bounced into the hotel, immediately making friends with everyone he set eyes upon. He was not still for one moment. After investigating our surroundings a bit, we got to bed around midnight American time. It would have been five o'clock in the morning in England, so the children had been awake almost twenty-four hours. They had more stamina than us!

Stefan was, unbelievably, awake and rushing about and waking us all up at ten to seven the next morning. Nobody could sleep after he was awake.

It was so hot and humid, but I was not complaining at all as I love the hot weather. How lovely it was to walk outside first thing and feel the sun bathing our bodies with golden warmth. We actually had to go indoors to get out of the heat, where the air conditioning kept the rooms lovely and cool. We walked up the promenade and found our apartment and discovered it had already been vacated, so we moved straight in after settling an extra day's money. What a lovely place it was, with two TVs, fridge/freezer, dishwasher, iron, Hoover and plenty of space! All the children rushed straight into the little outdoor pool while I unpacked.

Stefan was very hyperactive today. He climbed over a first floor balcony, walked down a canvas roof, which we realised later could have split at any time, and jumped from it straight into the swimming pool, some twelve feet or more below. He bit lumps from the polystyrene floats and spat them into the water, and then ran into the sea just below our apartment and caught a fish. When it was dead he placed it in the swimming pool. He pushed Louise into the pool twice, fully clothed each time. We were constantly worried for his and others' safety. Vaughan wanted to try his hand at fishing on a nearby pier, so he took Louise and Stefan. Relief for a few hours! Jane and I visited the local supermarket and were overwhelmed by the choice of things that we in England do not have. We bought basic provisions and spent far too long browsing around. We went back to the pier and discovered that Vaughan and the other two were not ready to leave, but Stefan was running amok, so I took him back to the apartment with Jane and me. That evening there were storms with so much lightning for hours on end that we sat outside the apartment in the sultry night air watching the rain tip down. Stefan crashed out at ten o'clock!

After several more sun-soaked days, we headed up the coast towards Orlando, some 250 miles north of Miami, and booked in at an Interstate Inn. Stefan was horrendous after such a long journey and went crazy, rushing around like a mad animal and jumping on all the beds. Vaughan ended up getting very angry with him and an unpleasant hour followed before bedtime. Stefan did not settle until around midnight, during which time we all became more and more frazzled as he kept everyone awake. I ended up having to share a bed with him and he thrashed about even in his sleep, giving me no more than three hours' sleep.

At six o'clock the next morning, after a most unpleasant night, the little darling was wide awake and made sure everyone else woke up too! They were all shattered. Somehow we managed to gather ourselves and our brood together and head off to the Magic Kingdom in Disneyland. Stefan caused grief the entire day as he just would not queue for the various rides and kept running off, making different excuses. I was worried for his safety as much as anything, as he lacks inhibition and was chatting to everyone and anyone and making blunt comments to complete strangers. Try as I might it was so difficult to keep tabs on him as he darted in and out among the throngs of people. At one point he dashed off and returned a few minutes later carrying a very large toy rifle which he was determined to keep by his side, even on all the rides.

Vaughan and the girls went on a ride together while Stefan and I waited for them, during which time he accidentally barged me in the mouth, splitting my lip quite badly. It bled a lot and I was in considerable pain for about an hour. My lip swelled up and I looked a sight! I was not going to let it spoil the rest of the day, though, so we stayed on until the Magic Kingdom closed at eleven, having our last rides and watching the spectacular floodlit parade and sampling the wonderful display of fireworks. Having had so little sleep the previous night and been woken so early by Stefan that morning, Louise, who was only nine, got beside herself with fatigue and ended up asleep on the kerbside in Main Street across Vaughan's lap as we sat watching the events, while Jane and Stefan bustled off to do some last minute shopping for souvenirs. By the time we emerged from the heavy traffic all leaving Disney at the same time, and returned to the Interstate Inn, it was almost one thirty in the early hours, and we collapsed into bed, exhausted. After more minor trouble with Stefan, with him yet again thrashing himself about in a temper on the bed, even he was too exhausted to argue much more and fell asleep.

Somewhere outside the apartment blocks the next day, Stefan saw two snakes and spent the next hour trying to catch them, getting into trouble with the management of the inn complex, as they were not sure how dangerous (if at all) they were. It did not deter him, and he kept returning to the place where they were and even tried to get them into a box. Oh, help! We drove to a place called 'Wet and Wild', which is a huge water park with the biggest flumes and chutes one has ever seen. As usual Stefan did not wish to conform and queue like everyone else, but did his 'own thing'. On one occasion Vaughan saw him scaling up the steps to one of the rides with an enormous blow-up whale on his back. Everyone else was using the provided mats but he was riding with a difference. Vaughan managed to intervene before disaster struck.

After our few wonderful days in Orlando, we returned to the apartment in Miami. Then Stefan went missing! A man who lived next door to the apartments where we were staying used to rent out 'banana' bikes, but was now retired. He told us he wanted to have a word with us about our son. Apparently that morning he had lent Stefan one of these bikes, and there had been four complaints from the public about his reckless driving. The police had turned up about another incident – a stolen, dumped car. Coincidentally he'd found Stefan, and he had matched the description given. The officer had given him a wigging.

The man (called Gary) then told us how dangerous it was for any child to be around alone. We had been told that this resort was very safe! He also said that Stefan was on his final warning with his banana bike. At this point, Stefan suddenly appeared on the bike. Gary took it from him, as he seemed unable to comply with his regulations. He also advised us not to let the children out of our sight, especially at night. We spoke to the children and warned them not to go off by themselves any more. Stefan, ignoring the warnings, slunk off.

The next thing was a call from the manageress of the Hollywood Resort where we were staying. Stefan had sneaked onto the roof and was throwing things down onto the path and the swimming pool below! Then shortly after the call he appeared with the security guard from the adjoining complex. He was very pleasant but explained that there had been a series of complaints and he had watched Stefan throw sticks and other things from the resort roof onto the path. That was *it*! Vaughan and I spoke extremely sternly to him and told him that no way was he going to go off on his own again.

The holiday shortly came to an end, and after several more hot and sunny days spent on the beach, in the pool, fishing and shopping and dining out, we finally reluctantly packed our bags, cleaned up the apartment and said our farewells. No doubt the resort breathed a sigh of relief to see us depart...

It had been a most delightful vacation and we felt blessed by the generosity of Vaughan's friend in lending us his apartment so that we could have the opportunity to have a holiday, even though it was fraught with Stefan's misdeeds and hyperactivity.

On holiday

13 JULY

Stefan broke a window in our front porch.

15 JULY

Stefan bought a catapult without my knowledge. The next day he smuggled it into school and hit a teacher's windscreen with it. He was suspended again.

20 JULY

He broke the kitchen window with a football.

August

I forgot to give Stefan his medication one Sunday. He became extremely restless during the church service. While my eyes were closed during the prayers, he rolled up little pieces of paper and stuck one behind my ear and put one in my hand, like a cigarette, and then stuck one up my nose. Vaughan walked out before the service ended.

The next week Stefan fractured his wrist falling off the top of the slide in our local park.

My sister took him out for dinner one evening to give me a break. He told the waitress she reminded him of Dracula. I am sure she was one happy lady that night!

September

Stefan acquired a zebra finch with his pocket money. He pulled the tail feathers from it. He wanted to make a quill. I was very distraught when I discovered the feathers missing. He denied it.

It was discovered a few days later that he had nicked the chainsaw from my brother-in-law's house. He said he had found the saw at the local park. It does not bear thinking about what could have happened if we had not discovered it very promptly. I try to be vigilant at all times, but at the same time I cannot keep him tied to the house, nor do I have eyes in the back of my head (although I have often told the children that I do!).

The first week back at school has not been good. Stefan flicked ink across the classroom, and punched a boy, making his nose bleed, according to the teacher. Apparently the boy had first provoked him and Stefan is very reactive, hitting out if provoked in any way. He was kept in isolation the entire day. There were a lot of other minor incidents throughout the first week.

Stefan and his best friend went out for hours on their bikes one day. They climbed over a locked timber yard to get some wood to build a den. Someone saw them and reported them. The police turned up and took their names. The friend's mother came by and explained. The police were very nice about it all. The next day Stefan disappeared for seven and a half hours while I was at work and his dad was in charge. At twelve years old it is becoming increasingly difficult to keep tags on him, as he sees his friends out and about and thinks he should have the same entitlement. He does not realise that he needs to be kept under stricter surveillance because of his attention deficit, and I try to let him have a little more freedom, but I know that he poses a risk to himself. It is so hard to strike a happy balance.

After school one day he went to see a friend. They asked an older boy to get a 'gat' gun that they had seen in a shop. Somehow they had got hold of £15 between them. Stefan wrapped it up and presented it to his dad for a 'present'. Somehow I thought this was a ploy for him to get the gun in his possession. Vaughan put it in his wardrobe overnight. But Stefan is no fool, and knew it was there. The next day he retrieved the gun and shot people with pellets from it. A neighbour over the road complained that he had shot at his boy. Vaughan was furious with Stefan and confiscated the gun immediately. He went across the road, apologised and made peace with the neighbour. He should have taken the gun right out of the house as soon as he had been given it. A couple of days later the police came round investigating another incident that had been reported involving the gun. Stefan had shot a pellet at a passer-by and it had hit her, but not badly, fortunately. I shudder to think what might have happened if he had hit her in the face, for instance. Oh, whatever next will my son do! It did not take long to find out.

He had an ink fight at school with a boy. He came home with his white shirt covered with ink. He then proceeded to throw glass all over our front driveway. It did not stop there. The next day he brought a field mouse home. I insisted he return it to the field by our house, explaining to him that it would need to find its own family and that it would not be happy with us. While I was dealing with this, I received a complaint from some people who live further up the road from us. Stefan had broken the chain surrounding their front garden by riding his bike straight through it. I took him up to apologise immediately. They were very nice about it.

A couple of days passed. Then my mum rang to say that Stefan had taken a crystal from her jewellery box. I increased Stefan's medication ever so slightly that day, having checked with the hospital that it was OK to do so. He was quite subdued for a while after school. He seemed to have no energy and no incentive to do anything, but he was awake until twelve thirty at night. I wondered whether it had been the right decision to increase the tablets. Sometimes I just did not know what to do for the best.

The next day I found out that Stefan had met up with some older boys. I found a packet of cigarettes in his trousers. Most of them had been smoked. He had brought home a hard-core porn magazine, and loads of condoms. It gets increasingly worrying.

He threw a stick at Louise and the pointed end just missed her eye by an inch. She sustained a large lump on her forehead. She cried herself to sleep.

The police came round to caution Stefan about the gun incident. No further action. Relief!

So he 'trimmed' the dog's tail!

He burnt Louise with the car cigarette lighter and punched her. He arranged all my jewellery in a box very nicely, and then shook the whole box up. He has taken to breaking pencils and throwing them everywhere. Why?

October

Stefan was suspended from school for the fourth time for messing around in the technology lesson and throwing a chisel. Why was he not getting the help and support that his statement of special educational needs said he should be having?

It was hard having him home all day while he was suspended as he always got into mischief. He found an old record player at our local tip and brought it home. He then found his dad's hammer and smashed it to smithereens. We made him clear up the mess. The following day he made a mixture of aftershave plus my perfume and some other stuff he found in the bathroom. He put some in an empty beer bottle and told Vaughan he had left his beer upstairs. Unawares, Vaughan took a huge swig. Yuk!

The next day he took a huge bag that he had stuffed with sleeping bags to make something vaguely like a punchbag and suspended it from the upstairs banisters so that it hung down right outside our lounge door. When Vaughan opened the door it swung out and hit him in the face. Vaughan chased him up the stairs in a temper, but Stefan locked himself in the bathroom. Between the pair of them they managed to break the lock while forcing the door open. There was plaster all over the landing. Sometimes – well, quite frequently, in fact – I despair of ever having even a semblance of normality in our house! Vaughan disappears more and more frequently for long periods of time. Maybe it is his way of coping with the stress!

November

Stefan was reinstated at school. He called his form teacher a big, fat b—d! He was put into isolation for three days.

He has another new obsession. This time it is badminton. He plays as much as he can, with whomever he can get hold of to give him a game. He has one or two friends who also enjoy playing. I am so pleased that this is a good obsession for once. Unfortunately, along with this, he also has a huge obsession with Parker pens. This week at school he was again put into isolation for another two days for taking a member of staff's Parker pen. He also likes anything glittery, like a magpie. I found that he had smuggled one of my rings into school, along with one of his sister's bracelets and three watches. They were all stuffed into his pockets.

13 NOVEMBER

He was suspended for the fifth time from school today for throwing a piece of Blu-tack across the classroom. Methinks the school really does not want him there, and now picks up on anything for an excuse to have me keep him at home. I telephoned the educational psychologist.

Meanwhile his obsession with Parker pens increased. With a little bit of pocket money that he earned, he went out and bought a set of pens. They had to be Parker pens. No ordinary ones would do.

I bought a second-hand computer for the three children. It was very cheap. They loved it. Stefan became terribly possessive of it. He did not want the girls to have their turn on it.

By the middle of November the time had come round for Stefan's monthly appointment at Great Ormond Street Hospital. He does not enjoy going, even though I try to make an interesting day for him after he has seen the specialist. He usually runs amok in the hospital, but they are used to children with all sorts of difficulties and are very understanding. The consultant usually checks his pulse, heart, weight and height and then we have a consultation, in which we report on what has been happening, how the medication is and receive further input, behaviour strategies to attempt, and everything is monitored. I told them about the continual suspension times from school and the lack of understanding and help received.

He is still suspended from school. The head teacher said that Vaughan and I could see him and the head of year the next day, but it was not convenient for Vaughan, so we suggested the following day. The head said he would confirm this. Meanwhile, all the days when Stefan is at home, he is receiving no education.

I took Stefan with me to do my weekly shop at the supermarket. He wandered off by himself. I was called by the security guards a while later. He had been caught shoplifting... Parker pens! We were escorted into a back office. I became extremely distraught and burst into tears. 'How could you do this, Stefan?' I sobbed. Stefan went very quiet. He was let off with a warning. The staff management could see how greatly this had upset me. During the drive home, he was very quiet. I think he got his punishment by seeing how upset it had made me. When we arrived home he put all my shopping away. I guess this was his way of trying to make amends.

20 NOVEMBER

We were supposed to be meeting the head teacher along with the head of year. We received no word from the school at all. I decided to write a letter to the Board of Governors and to the educational psychologist. I really have had enough.

21 NOVEMBER

Stefan cleaned the house today. He polished everything in sight, including all my apples. I went to eat one later, before I realised what he had done. It tasted of polish but it was certainly nice and shiny!

22 NOVEMBER

He dressed up as a young lady with high heels, make-up, a wig and handbag. He knocked on the front door. For one long moment I did not realise it was him, he looked so authentic!

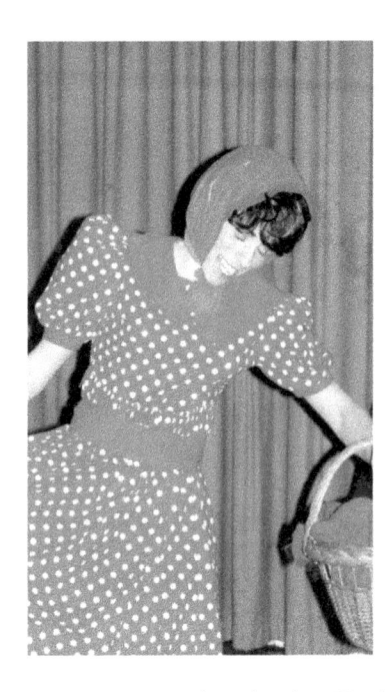

Dressing up as 'Little Red Riding Hood'

23 NOVEMBER

He decorated a waste-paper bin by covering it with paper and drawing a large face on it and attaching a wig. He made a long body which he managed to attach to the bin, making a sort of witch-like creature which he then dangled from the upstairs window, so that it slowly swung up and down and side to side past our downstairs lounge window outside. Talk about another 'Just William'!

24 NOVEMBER

He is still out of school! I am seriously contemplating home education.

I went into Stefan's bedroom one morning late in the month to find that he had bashed his bedroom windowpane out. He had thrown lumps of glass out of the gap all over next door's lawn.

December

He is back at school! He has been given a new timetable and is dropping some academic subjects temporarily. He has also been assigned more one-to-one help.

Not a day too soon!

29 DECEMBER

I took all three children to the cinema just after Christmas. Stefan threw a whole cup of ice cubes from the top foyer down to the ground floor over the balcony.

1998

We were on one of our monthly journeys to London to see the specialist at Great Ormond Street Hospital. As we stepped off the underground train, Stefan enquired, 'Mum, why do all the dogs have to go to Liverpool Street?'

I was puzzled by this question so I asked him, 'What do you mean?'

'Well, I heard the man over the loudspeaker say, "Alsations to Liverpool Street",' he replied. (All stations!)

Another time, and another journey on the underground to the same place and Stefan and I were in a carriage full of commuters, tightly packed like sardines. Stefan carefully studied the grim faces, some reading newspapers or books or magazines, others staring blankly into space or watching out for their stations, but most sitting or standing in silence. He started to talk to one or two of them, asking them where they were going or what they were doing, much to my British embarrassment, aware that they might find this young boy irritating, but also never quite sure what he might say in his disinhibited fashion. Suddenly, true to form, he blurted out in a loud voice, 'Come on, you lot, stop looking so miserable and cheer up!' I couldn't fit under the seat, but I would have crawled under if there was room! To my utter amazement, everyone started grinning, then laughing, and within minutes, people were talking and chatting to one another and by the time we stepped off that train, conversations were flowing and the whole atmosphere had lightened up. As we stepped off, Stefan turned round and called out, 'Now *that*'s better! Goodbye, everyone!' He certainly brightens up the world in his unique way!

Some years previously, Vaughan and I had joined a support group, and from time to time we all met up and we also attended various national conferences and information sessions to learn all we could about the condition. It was also very helpful to be able to talk with other parents who had a child with ADHD and to share experiences and give one another encouragement, although I came to realise fairly early on that Stefan was probably by far the most challenging and outrageous case. It was one particular day at the end of March that such a meeting took place and I went along. One of the best things about all meeting together with our children was that there was an acceptance of each other's kids when they 'played up' or displayed severely antisocial behaviour, because we all understood how difficult it was in public places. Here, there was a sense of safety and acceptance that no one was tut-tutting when our dear little rogues all but climbed the walls! Having lost friends over the years because of our son's extreme behaviour, it was nice to know that in the group we felt accepted and not judged; something many of the parents had felt too.

On this particular occasion we met in a local public house which had a family area. We ordered our food and drinks and chatted among ourselves while the little darlings played or fought with one another. Shortly, the manager came over and wanted to know who the owner of the little blond boy was. Here we go again, I thought to myself, as I shrank down in my chair. One of the barmaids was crying. Stefan had upset her by calling her all sorts of names. Every time she had emerged from the kitchens with both hands full with a customer's order, he had stood blocking her way. When she had asked him to move each time, he would not let her through until she said 'please'. I apologised. Luckily the manager knew why we were there as a group and was sympathetic.

1999

January/February

Stefan is not unwell very often but he recently had a short, sharp attack of flu. As he was not able to have his medication during this time, he went absolutely wild, dashing about and throwing things and hitting out and being completely daft. He broke a huge glass picture frame on purpose and got the cheese out of the fridge and put slices between his toes and was generally out of control. I now know how awful his behaviour is without medication. A few days later, he made a barbecue with half a bottle of white spirit. He found an old rag and tied it to a stick and set light to it with more white spirit. There were a lot of flames and I was distraught that he could manage to do these things in such a short space of time, when I was upstairs seeing to the youngest child or merely just in the bathroom. The next day he came home for lunch from school with his friend and threw an egg out of his bedroom window.

We had decided to give him a mobile phone this year for Christmas to make him feel more on a par with his friends. He had been thrilled to bits with it, but we hoped and prayed that he would not misuse it. Well, of course, that was maybe too much to expect. Sure enough, and unbeknown to us, he had been harassing a girl from school whom he had taken a huge fancy to, and had been calling her many times from his mobile, to the extent that she had apparently reported this to her parents, who had contacted the police directly. It made me wonder – why did they not first contact us so that we could have dealt with it ourselves instead of running to the police? If I had an issue with a child, I would always first seek to sort it out with the parents. As it was, we had to go to the police station with Stefan to make a statement after he had been 'arrested'. He had his phone confiscated; something that Vaughan and I would have done anyway, had we known the facts.

During February, we visited our family 'down under'. Stefan was due to have a drug respite, as advised by his consultant, so we decided that this would be the best time, when he did not need to concentrate on schoolwork and he would have open spaces to run about in rather than our confined built-up area, which is usually a recipe for disaster of some sort or another. Stefan loved Australia. He did upset one poor old gentleman on the beach one day, who made some comment about why weren't the children in school. This was like a red rag to a bull for Stefan, and he consequently took umbrage and threw a bucket of water over the sunbathing man.

There was one other unfortunate incident which clouded the rest of my holiday as it was so traumatic. We were high up in the Blue Mountains with our family and my uncle and aunt. I was watching Stefan carefully as we picked our way gingerly along the very narrow mountain paths, working our way higher and higher to reach the spectacular views from the lookout places. Stefan and his sister were lagging behind and I voiced my concerns about him, knowing full well that he has little sense of danger. I was told not to worry so much, so I buttoned my mouth and thought, Maybe I'm just being too fussy.

By this time we had reached a good height and, gazing down from our lookout, the trees below looked just like sprigs of broccoli, they were so far down. Stefan and his sister were way below. Suddenly, without any warning we heard Vaughan's urgent command booming out at the top of his voice, '*Stefan, get back now!*'

He had taken off his socks and shoes and had ventured under a barrier where a waterfall was running over the side of the mountain and was paddling just feet away from the edge. One slip on the slimy rocks and he would have been sucked over the edge to his death hundreds of feet below. My legs gave way underneath me and I shook so much I had to be steadied. My uncle hastily retreated down the paths to retrieve Stefan, who fortunately had obeyed his dad (for once!), probably hearing the urgency in his voice. He received a good ticking off from my uncle, who then kept him under his wing for the remainder of the trek. Stefan could not understand what all the fuss was about and could not for the life of him realise the danger he had put himself in, protesting that he knew he was all right.

That night as I lay in bed, my mind kept replaying the whole scenario, and the seriousness of what it could have ended up like reduced me to crying silent ears. I think I was also in shock. Even today, whenever I recount the story, I am filled with the horror of how close we had come to losing him over the edge.

Stefan continued his challenging behaviour throughout the remainder of our time in Sydney and became obsessional about various things, especially about getting a surfboard, and also constantly tapping people on the shoulder, which became irritating. He wound his sisters up in various ways and interrupted conversations or played too roughly, annoying the girls endlessly. On the other hand, he slept better than he did at home, and he ate and ate and ate, consequently putting on quite a few extra pounds in weight. We celebrated his fourteenth birthday with him and we bought him a few Australian antiques that he could easily pack in his suitcase and bring back with him, as he loves to collect antiques and has become quite knowledgeable.

Stefan and Dad at Perry's Lookdown in the Blue Mountains

We arrived back in Britain at the end of February, after a stopover in Bali, where he bought bows and arrows from the beach peddlers. I was completely against this as, knowing him like I do, it could only spell trouble. Somehow they got back with us, and within days he had shot and killed his pet zebra finch, totally denying the misdeed and showing no remorse whatsoever. The following day he got hold of his younger sister in two pressure points each side of her neck, causing her to cry so much that I put him in his room for a while to cool off.

During that first week back from Australia we were all haywire in our sleeping patterns, especially Stefan, who kept falling asleep each evening at about six o'clock and waking up at four in the morning. Several times he would go out at this time, sometimes taking the dogs into the field which is almost next door to our house. Another day he arrived back with a loaf of bread and said he had bought it. Later on in the week he admitted he had taken it from someone's doorstep, where it had been left by the milkman. He also confessed that he had rather enjoyed going round the neighbourhood in the early hours and making little nicks in milk bottle tops and taking swigs of milk from the bottles.

We were advised to keep Stefan on a low dose of his medication for a while, as his body needed to gradually adjust. The school (and us!) certainly knew it! They were having a difficult time with him on his return. He had taken a swipe at a female pupil who had slapped him back round the face and he was put into isolation. He was suspended a few days later for an entire afternoon for calling a teacher 'a slut'. He made 'bombs' at home with our table tennis balls and burnt a hole in our dining room carpet. One evening I found him sitting in our front garden inside our beach wind shelter with two candles lit, but sitting ankle deep in *mud*! In spite of the antics, which virtually went on incessantly day and night, we did find that after the first week of adjusting to jet lag he was sleeping better and for longer periods. This was the first time in his life.

It was about this time that he decided he wanted a laptop computer and had managed to obtain £40 for a deposit on a second-hand one he had seen. He became obsessed with making enough money for the remaining £100. I took him to an antiques centre several miles away one day where he set up his own stall and managed to sell £20 worth of stuff that he had accumulated. By fair means or foul, soon he had acquired the money to purchase his laptop. The following Monday he went back to the second-hand shop where the man said to him that if he waited for a couple more days he would install 'Windows' for him. Stefan, being ever impulsive, could not wait, and took it home. He proceeded to take the back off the machine and fiddle with the electrics until it was completely broken, and was then mortified that it no longer worked.

March

We had decided to get a quote for redecorating Stefan's room, and the decorator arrived and I showed him the bedroom. While we were discussing the job, the doorbell rang again and Stefan rushed down to answer the door. It was a gentleman from our church. Stefan rushed back upstairs and said to the decorator, 'My mum's next customer has just arrived and is waiting downstairs. She's a prostitute!'

I was presented with the most gorgeous bunch of daffodils for Mother's Day. The rascal had been down to a nearby boulevard where they were growing in great clusters and had picked them. A couple of days later he found a large cardboard box and set fire to it in our front garden. He had also lit many candles all around the garden. He has quite a fascination with fire and lighting things which, as I have mentioned previously, accompanies many children and young people who have ADHD.

The next day, Stefan told me he was going up the road to visit his friend. I was quite pleased as I needed to go to my younger daughter's parents' evening at the school. It was virtually an impossible mission to ever attempt to take Stefan with me to anything like this, as he always created such havoc wherever we went, causing embarrassment, with other parents quick to express their disapproval of his behaviour. Life was often difficult for the girls in this respect, as they never felt they could invite friends round because of how he would behave, or I would have to try and find ways round the various events that occurred in the school calendar for each of them which would cause the least disruption to them. So I was pleased that he was going to visit this friend, and knew the mum would be watching out for him. She liked Stefan.

However, on my return, there was chaos outside the house. Stefan had decided to return home and had managed to climb up onto the apex of our roof and had tried to do a balancing act by walking along it. He had also lain down along the pinnacle, precariously balancing his body across the top. A neighbour had seen him and had alerted another neighbour, who had come round with a very long ladder to help get him down. I was horrified. He could so easily have slipped and been killed or severely injured. Once again, his apparent disregard for danger and his need for excitement had somehow given him the notion to attempt such a daredevil feat. Quite coincidentally, the following day we heard that a well-known entertainer had fallen off his roof and been killed, which shocked the nation.

I battled with so many thoughts during this time of Stefan's life. I knew that it was not safe to leave him alone, yet I also realised that he was now fourteen years old and he needed to be steered towards independence. It was to be a very difficult juggling act, which was to prove increasingly difficult and challenging over the next few years. Stefan longed to be treated the same as his friends, and yet I had to be vigilant enough to keep a close guard.

Because my husband has always struggled with his own problems (which have given rise to a specialist's diagnosis that they were what his son had, which is largely an inherited condition) he often found it almost impossible to cope with a son who displayed such severity of ADHD, and his way of dealing with it was not to! He would just 'be delayed' at the snooker club which was his 'cave' of respite, understandable in such circumstances, but I confess I was not always so understanding when he just did not show up often until very late on in the evening when the children were all in bed. Needless to say, I had to take Stefan with me when it was the parents' evening at his school during this month. And what happened? He threw a large stone at a teacher walking outside the building, narrowly missing her head.

Stefan continued to display quite wild behaviour over the ensuing days and we had to increase his medication back to the original dose. He was kept in isolation time after time at school – in fact it seemed that he spent more time alone than with his classmates. Vaughan and I realised that it was extremely challenging for the school to have a child like Stefan there, repeatedly causing chaos through his bizarre behaviour, and that they had to serve the needs of the other pupils who were anxious to learn and who could be held back by the time it could take to calm a class down once he had caused disruption. Constantly, I felt I was 'fighting the system' to get more support from the special needs department. Although he had been given a statement of special educational needs, which established that he should have one-to-one support throughout the day, he was only allocated one hour each morning, which was completely inadequate. We knew that the funding had been granted for more hours – sixteen in all – but he was not given it and was then suspended or kept in isolation as a punishment when he 'messed up' when not with a learning support helper.

It seemed very unfair, as the child desperately needed this help. In fact we understood from his specialist at Great Ormond Street Hospital that he had a particularly severe form of ADHD. We went into the school on many occasions to speak with the head teacher, but we both had the feeling that Stefan was not really wanted there and that they made little effort to understand the nature of this disorder, apart from one or two members of staff. I even went to great lengths to obtain some information for them about ADHD, with tips specifically designed to help teachers cope with having such a pupil. I had the notes all photocopied, enough for many of the teachers at the school who had dealings with Stefan. I took them into the school and delivered them to the office. I learnt later that the notes were never given out to the named teachers; they were disregarded and probably destroyed.

Because he had thrown the stone at a teacher during parents' evening, we were in no doubt that he might well be suspended, possibly permanently. We felt we were living on a knife edge, waiting for the school to find a way to get him out. We were not blind to the other side of the equation, and realised that it must be very difficult to try to educate a class of pupils when one of the children had such severe behaviour problems as Stefan.

Just as we thought, he was excluded from the school the following week. This would have repercussions in so many ways – one of them being a cause for concern as to what I would do with him when I went out to do my part-time job as a swimming teacher. I was well aware that he really could not be left alone at all, but it seemed I now had little option until I could reorganise things. So I went, and fortunately on this particular day it was only a short period of time, but I was still uneasy. I got back as quickly as I possibly could to find – *chaos!* He had got every single toy out from every room in the house, and he had gone into the kitchen and tried to make candles by melting down others, and there was candle wax everywhere!

That night he was wide awake until way past one o'clock in the morning. The next morning, my mother offered to take him out for a short while to give me a break. He took £1 out with him that no doubt he found (or stole) from somewhere, and bought ten bars of chocolate for 10p each, and had downed the lot before my mother could stop him.

During the Easter holidays, I took the children down to Kent, to stay at my sister and brother-in-law's holiday chalet near Deal, right on the coast. It is lovely and peaceful there and the children can play outside on the grass with no fear of any traffic, and there are lots of places to visit and things to do. The site has a swimming pool and a clubhouse where there is nightly entertainment and where the children can dance and join in some fun and games. The site managers and staff know our family, and I guess their hearts must sink a little when they see our family appear again with Stefan, although they also do like him because he keeps them entertained with his antics. The first evening we wandered down to the clubhouse where Stefan went to chat to some of the bar staff. Later I was told he was blurting out things about prostitution and other seedy subjects. It makes me wonder if people think that we teach such things to our children!

The next day, Stefan was sent out of the swimming pool by the manager. That day he also shovelled sand into the mouth of a little boy whom he was playing with and the child nearly choked. Stefan said he was 'only playing'. That same evening I had a game of pool with him, and suddenly he turned round and clouted Louise hard on the leg with his snooker cue. I did not finish the game I was playing with him but immediately took him back to the chalet. The following day I took the children to visit an old friend of mine who lived about an hour's drive from the chalet. While we were there, Stefan punched Louise really hard on the leg, making her cry a lot. I sent him to sit in the car for five minutes 'to cool off'. It makes life difficult when one cannot even visit friends for a short while without him 'erupting'. When we got back to the chalet he threw a large stone which only just missed the chalet window, so once again he was banished inside for half an hour.

The next day we drove home and went down to the seafront to a funfair. The children loved going on the various rides but Stefan kept spitting all the time. He spat while the rides went up high and I am sure some of it landed on the poor unsuspecting people beneath. For his finale, he got thrown off a water flume ride as he was ascending on the *outside* of the structure.

On 20 April we received a letter informing us that he had been expelled from his school permanently. That week he made a fire in our side passage, and the next week he and a neighbour's child lit some paper just around the corner from our house. Two people had seen them and reported the incident to the police. I wondered how I was going to manage with him home all day and every day. At least I had a few hours' reprieve while he was at school. Now even that was gone.

All three children have piano lessons – yes, including Stefan! After several years with one piano teacher, she finally informed me that she could no longer cope with him but could recommend a colleague who would be willing to take him on. Stefan spent more time under or on top of her piano than playing it, or he would go off on a tangent 'doing his own thing', to the exasperation of his teacher. Many a time I went to fetch him and was greeted by the teacher all red-faced and frazzled-looking, and sometimes I felt just a little guilty that I had ever asked her to take him on, but not quite guilty enough to withdraw him altogether. Apart from giving me a half-hour break – and you've no idea how precious even half an hour was – I knew that Stefan had inherited some form of musical ability, as he only had to hear a tune a few times and he would accurately play a rendition on the piano. But it was always a marathon task trying to get him to do any piano practice, and I would try anything and everything from reasoning (impossible) and bribery to begging, pleading, arguing, and even getting angry; but it had little impact and he tried my patience to the very limit.

I never left him to do his practice by himself. That would not have happened. I always took the time to sit with him and go through everything, with him playing up, belting out his own tunes, messing about or generally being disruptive. I refused to give up. Between us, the piano teacher and I worked as a team and eventually, after extraordinary efforts from us both, we managed to nurture him through Grades One, Two, and Three.

May

Very occasionally, my mum and dad would come to babysit so that Vaughan and I could have an evening out with friends. One such evening we returned home to find my dad wild-eyed and ferocious. They had had a bad evening with Stefan, and he was not one to tolerate his challenging behaviour. The next evening Stefan stayed awake all night and went out at four o'clock in the morning. He posted 'Happy Birthday' posters down the entire length of our road. We only knew of this when we were awoken at six o'clock by the sound of banging, and looking out of our bedroom window we saw him on our front driveway banging nails into some wood which he had decorated. It was my birthday that day, and he had thought he would do something special for me.

By nine in the morning, I was shattered, but we had arranged to go out to a little place in the countryside. Stefan was dreadful on both journeys to and from the place, winding his younger sister up mercilessly until Vaughan finally flipped. The rest of the day was chaos. Vaughan had ended up smacking Stefan for being rude to him back at home, and he had run out of the house and Louise had become very upset. It was not a happy ending to my birthday.

Is there no end to what Stefan turns up at the house with? Any old furniture that he sees dumped anywhere he brings home. Wardrobes, dining tables, a sideboard, even a grandfather clock. He has brought stuff back on our wheelbarrow. Then one day he arrived home with an old moped. He said that his friend had 'sold' it to him.

A local policeman came round to the house one day. He said that someone in the neighbourhood had complained that Stefan had lit some paper outside their house and had nearly set fire to their fence. Later on in the week he sprayed a whole canister of shaving foam onto some paper and had set light to it in the middle of the flat piece of roof outside Louise's bedroom. During conferences I attended over the years, I learned that children with ADHD usually display an inordinate fascination with fire, generally because of the 'buzz' factor.

Every month our appointment comes through for Great Ormond Street Hospital. Stefan hates going. This month we discussed his medication. The specialist wanted to try him with a different medication – Respiridone. He thought it might help with his poor sleeping patterns. The following week we started him on quite a low dose. It only made a marginal difference.

Stefan has now embarked on a junk food diet. I don't know whether this is in direct rebellion to the normally healthy diet I have always given all three children, as I am aware that too many unhealthy foods can affect us in so many ways and therefore have been quite careful in ensuring they have no added sugar in their diets, as well as nutritional balance. I made a note of what Stefan ate in one particular day when we visited Colchester Zoo and he had some money on him.

> 9 a.m. – two pieces of bread spread thickly with peanut butter.
>
> Yoghurt with candy bits he bought at the garage en route, washed down with a large bag of sweets and a fizzy drink.
>
> 1 p.m. – two peanut butter sandwiches. Doughnut. Ice cream. One ice lolly straight after. One large Refresher bar.
>
> Mid-afternoon – two cheeseburgers. More sweets.

5 p.m. – McDonald's cheeseburger and chips followed by ice cream sundae.

On arrival at home – more sandwiches.

Maybe it's the change of medication!

Stefan has 'antique' shops on our front lawn nearly every day at the moment. He is becoming quite knowledgeable about antiques. When he is a little older maybe I will be able to find an antiques course he can attend. Sometimes I take him to the Broadway, where he will spend an afternoon going round all the antique dealers and the shops. They all know Stefan and he seems to be popular with them. I went in with him to one shop and the dealer in there told me what a charming and polite boy he is. *Wow!* How lovely, after all the negative comments that we hear so often. He is obsessed with picture frames at the moment. Sometimes he goes to the Broadway all by himself, wandering around the antique shops and wheeling and dealing, and arrives home with an odd assortment of old paintings and dirty old frames that he lovingly pores over. In addition, I have lost count of the number of my pictures he has pulled apart for the frames alone. Because he also loves to play with knives and any other dangerous equipment, he has taken all my kitchen knives. Nothing is safe from his hands. All my polishes, glue, tapes, hammer and nails have disappeared. Oh, not to mention all the food he nicks from the cupboards!

Vaughan said he does not want Stefan to do any more 'shops' on our front lawn. Stefan stole £2 out of my purse and went to the shops early one morning and bought £2 worth of 1p sweets. No pocket money that week! He went up into the attic and took a whole lot of old photos that belonged to my grandmother, along with some old documents. I was not pleased. If only he had asked.

At the weekend, I took Stefan to an Antiques Fayre. He bought two swords and an old gat gun. I had to take him back to the man who had sold them to him and get a refund. He continues to have such a fascination with swords, guns, fire… in fact anything dangerous! The following day he made a fire in his shoes and another fire with paper outside our church. Earlier during the service at church he had used a laptop computer and written some very rude words and phrases in large letters and held them up at the back for everyone to see.

A fire officer visited this month regarding the amount of small fires that he had started over the past weeks. Stefan was to start a fire course on a one-to-one basis. I was so pleased. He is also starting some home education from the end of this month for five hours a week, which is just one hour per day. It's better than nothing, I suppose.

June

Stefan was so desperate to earn some money that he recently took on a paper round. He conscientiously put the various leaflets that came with the papers inside each one, and with his younger sister's help donned his roller skates and set off on his round each week. He was delighted with the extra money. It lasted less than three weeks before he tired of it. Being sensible and good was just too much. Instead he learned that if he put on his dad's spiked metal golf shoes and rode his bike very fast, while scraping the shoes along the pavement, he could make sparks fly. When his dad found out there were more sparks flying!

We discovered three small holes had been drilled through our bathroom door. Was it to peep? A few days later he bashed the wall in the side passage outside our house with an old hammer that he had bought at a car boot sale along with a box full of other old tools. He had hit the wall so hard that the whole downstairs toilet system cracked inside the interior wall and water flooded from it, making it unusable. Vaughan and I were *not* happy!

The recent new medication that had been prescribed for Stefan had made some difference to his sleeping patterns, after persisting with it over a period of weeks, and we noticed that he was going to sleep before midnight as opposed to the early hours. One day I forgot to give him this new medication and he was up most of the night, having decided to clean his roller skates, taking all the wheels and bearings off. The bathroom carpet and basin and everywhere he had touched had got covered in black grease by the time I found him in the early hours. I was very cross and very tired and very fed up. He then used up all the rolls of toilet paper trying to clean up until I got him out of the bathroom and into his bedroom, where he continued to polish his skates and fiddle about, even though I took his light bulb out in an attempt to get him to settle.

The next evening he decided on another mission. He would do some gardening for me. He mowed both front and back lawns, then decided to trim my prize plant and cut all the leaves to two-thirds their original sizes. I found that he had also dug out an oval shape from the front lawn and planted a small bush in the middle, which he had dug up from our rockery. I really tried hard to be pleased and praise him for his 'ingenuity' so as not to discourage his 'artistic' approach, while biting my tongue hard.

Continuing with his unusual ingenious ways, he bought home an old cocktail cabinet that he had found and shifted home somehow. Inside, he found a pair of cufflinks, and went straight off and sold them to a lady, making himself £10 richer. A few days later a very old commode arrived home with him. Really, whatever next would be brought home? I was beginning to feel like Steptoe and Son, with our house being turned into a dumping ground of dilapidated old furniture. The next day he took all his cash out of his building society and came home with a stone bird bath which he had bought on impulse for his dad, then went out and purchased nearly £10 worth of sweets, which he filled the bird bath with. It was now adorning our hallway!

Just to make a change, Stefan disappeared into the woods which were almost opposite our house. He went off on Louise's bike with some friends one day. He arrived home some time later completely covered from head to toe in thick mud, with just a pair of eyes peeping out at me. It took a long time in the bath to get himself cleaned up.

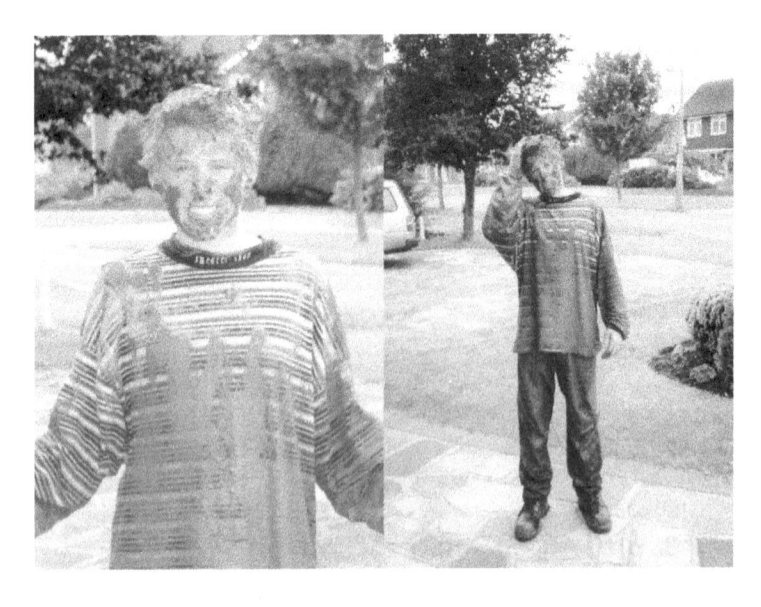

After one of Stefan's 'walks' in the woods!

Vaughan had been decorating his room, putting some wooden panelling up and varnishing it. Stefan decided his dad needed a helping hand, so using a pair of new white sports socks for a paintbrush, he 'helped' varnish a panel.

Over the next few days I noticed that Stefan had become very moody and quite obnoxious at bedtimes, often going to bed in a very aggressive frame of mind, refusing to say goodnight to us, and being argumentative and rude. I went into his room to say goodnight and he told me to p— off and threw his portable CD player across the room. The next night he was the same, rowing with Vaughan and then being rude to me as well. He had a most aggressive attitude and threw things across the room. In the end I got very angry with him and smacked him on the arm. He flew out of bed and threw me across the room. He is bigger than me now. He always seems to cause confrontations last thing at night, and it ends up horribly. Vaughan has been taking him to play tennis in the evenings to try and channel some of this aggressive behaviour, and Stefan has become very good at tennis and often beats his dad. He has been playing most evenings lately; sometimes my sister and a friend join them up on the local tennis courts for a foursome, and occasionally I have played too.

July

A letter arrived from the education department. They want Stefan back in a mainstream school and named the school. They then telephoned us to say there had been a mistake and it was the wrong school and he would have to go to the catchment one. I told them that two children with ADHD had been expelled from there and that no way was Stefan going to be the third. He was not going to be set up to fail. We shall see what happens now.

Stefan saw a suspension bike in a second-hand shop where he had bought a rubbish laptop. He tried it out. It clonked badly. The dealer said a slight adjustment was needed. After the experience with the laptop I did not intend buying anything electrical or anything that moved from this particular shop ever again. Stefan badly wanted it. I said absolutely no. He went on and on about it, becoming obsessed with the idea of getting the bike, even though I told him it would be useless. Day after day after day he would obsess about it, going on and on. So he decided to 'borrow' Jane's bike one day, and instead of putting it back afterwards, he dumped it down behind our car. I did not see it as I backed out of our driveway and drove right over it, buckling the wheel. Poor Jane!

About this time, I took Stefan to his first auction. He was fascinated. He had taken along a tea set that he had purchased from one of his second-hand shops. It was to be auctioned off, and he was delighted when it had sold. A few days later it transpired that he had been to the shop that had the clonking bike for sale and put a deposit on it with the money he had got from the sale of the tea set!

One evening an elderly friend called to see us. He wore a heart pacemaker and Stefan was interested to hear about this. Jane was playing a piece of music on the piano that she had composed and asked our friend if he could think of a suitable title for it. 'I know,' piped up Stefan, 'call it "Pacemaker"!'

Stefan was now working towards the Grade Four exam with

his piano lessons. Oh, how *hard* it still was to get him to practise! He always refused to, and I still had to beg, bribe, plead, and get nasty before he eventually condescended to do some, with me sitting by his side. He just scraped through this last exam, and by then the teacher and I realised we had reached a limit with him and could not push him any further. Apart from which, more and more he was opting to play tunes from memory. Nowadays he still plays from memory only, but has quite a repertoire of tunes that he will sit and play for hours. He listens to a piece of music and then plays it by ear, which is where his musical ability lies, but I do not regret the time and effort over the early years of his life to introduce him to the fundamentals of music.

One of the reasons I invested so much time and energy into music with the children was because they come from a musical background on both sides of the family. My own father was a wonderful pianist, as were my grandfather and uncle, and on Vaughan's side there was musical ability also. I can play a little too, and I wanted to encourage all three children to pursue music to reach their own potentials. Jane finished all eight grades and has a huge love of all kinds of music now that she is an adult, playing the keyboard at church, the 'hang' drum, and several other instruments. Louise finished six grades, but the one who sits at the piano the most nowadays is Stefan!

It became more difficult to have people round to our house when Stefan got older, as there would always be repercussions, but one afternoon I held a prayer group meeting at ours. I used to have to pop out and check things were OK quite frequently, knowing the mischief that he would get up to when unsupervised. This particular afternoon I went to check on things and found that the little darling had cut a huge hole in a pair of his shorts. He had also tied the sash on Louise's dress to the kitchen chair, and she was stuck. The following afternoon he went round to a neighbour and came back with his hair all shorn off. That same day another neighbour came round to complain that Stefan had jumped right out in the middle of the road in front of his wife's car, giving her a terrible fright as she swerved to avoid running him over. He was livid.

I always felt on tenterhooks when Stefan was out and about on his 'travels', not knowing quite what he would get up to, and dreading a knock on my door with news that either he had hurt someone, or himself, or some other catastrophe. It was one such day that he went off to the beach with some friends and came back several hours later and told us, 'I think I've killed an on old lady.' As I tried to carefully question him, I hid the rising panic inside. Oh my gosh, supposing this was true? According to him, he had thrown a stone while on the beach and it had hit an old lady on the head. She had keeled over and was still lying there. I think maybe we would have heard more if this story had been true. I sincerely hope it was a gross exaggeration on his part! I decided not to go and check it out.

Towards the end of July I had to take Stefan to Great Ormond Street Hospital for the usual monthly appointment. This time the consultant wanted to run some tests without him being on his medication. I knew what that meant – a day of disinhibited behaviour! True to form, he started talking to everyone in the street. I tried to divert his attention. 'Look at that nice aristocratic gentleman, Stefan,' I remarked as we were walking towards an incredibly smartly dressed elderly man. As we passed by him, Stefan blurted out in a loud voice, 'My mum fancies you!'

On the underground train a man who was extremely dark-skinned came and sat down next to us. Stefan started making monkey noises in the back of his throat. Later on during the train journey home, he said in a very loud voice, 'Mum, you're an old cow what doesn't give milk any more,' and, pointing to a man across the gangway, added, 'and he's a male cow what's gone wrong!'

The last few days of July were brilliantly hot and sunny. Stefan and his friend spent long hours on the beach most days and there seemed to be no problems for a change. He spent one night at his friend's house, and in return, his friend came to us the following night and they sat happily watching a James Bond movie without any trouble, which was a relatively unusual occurrence and most pleasant. We were going to a church camp the following day and Stefan even managed to help me carry the luggage to the car. Another unusual gesture!

People in our church were mostly very tolerant of our son,

and we had some very positive comments about him during our camping week, in which hundreds of people from all over Britain joined together to worship, receive Bible teaching and ministry and to have fun. Only one person came up and told Vaughan and me how awful they thought Stefan was, and that his life was heading in the wrong direction, which only served to make me feel quite despondent. Stefan had tried lighting fires on the site, which was forbidden, with a whole box of live matches that somehow he had managed to get hold of and had built into a pyramid. I had found him just as he was about to light them and managed to kick them out of the way.

Being a nice-looking boy, Stefan began to attract the attention of one or two young females, and one in particular took a shine to him – and he to her. Within a couple of days they were wandering around the campsite with arms wrapped around each other, and popping across to visit each other's family tents! When the week came to an end there were promises to visit each other and hugs and kisses. Stefan was 'in love'!

We went to see my parents when we returned to tell them all about our week away. Stefan nicked something from their house while we were there, and later that evening my mum turned up at our house and gave him a good talking-to.

August

Stefan and I were interviewed by a reporter from *The Sunday Times* newspaper in relation to ADHD and promoting general public awareness. The feature appeared the following week.

I forgot to give Stefan his tablets one morning. The inevitable repercussions followed. He became almost unbearable, teasing Louise, making stupid noises, throwing things in his room and being totally out of focus. My parents came to lunch, and during the meal he told my dad that I was a cow. My father, being of the 'old school', told him off in no uncertain manner and was angry with him. Stefan ended up walking off and I had to explain to my dad that he was more verbally uninhibited without his medication. Another mealtime ruined.

To try and ease the situation I suggested that we all drove over to an antiques centre, with the girls as well. Stefan came with us and he wandered off to look at all the stalls, being as always fascinated with antiques. Some time later he returned carrying a really ancient and very sharp sword. I told him 'no way'. A big argument in the car park followed, and I insisted he took it back. He refused to tell me from which stall he got it from so I had to go back and ask each stallholder until I found the man who had sold it to him and returned it. Stefan was furious. Afternoon ruined.

I found out that Stefan had been bothering our neighbours, sometimes knocking on their door four times in one morning and not leaving until they had to be rude to him. He often takes our eggs from the fridge and finds novel things to do with them. Like using Vaughan's golf club to hit them into the road, or popping them whole into drinks, or casually lobbing them over our fence into next door's garden, or throwing them at neighbours' houses – or at people. One day when I had put the washing on I found that 'someone' had even put an egg in the washing machine and all the clothes were covered in eggshell. Maybe I should stop buying eggs…

I discovered three new holes in Jane's bedroom ceiling where Stefan had bored through with a drill. That's ours, the hall, the downstairs toilet door, the bathroom door and hers – all ruined. There was a terrible fracas at home in the evening with Vaughan and Stefan shouting at each other. Stefan argues all the time with either Louise or Vaughan, and now Vaughan spends most of the time out of the house. I suppose he cannot cope. He tried to tell Stefan that after a day's work he wants to come home to peace and quiet, but it usually ends up nasty, with insults flying around and total mayhem.

Stefan has a new suspension bike. He is delighted with it. I soon wondered whether it was such a good idea. He is so dangerous on it. His friends all have bikes and skateboards, and quite naturally he wants to be the same as they are. My neighbour told me that he had darted out on his bike right in front of her car, causing her to brake very sharply. When I addressed the issue with Stefan later on, and tried to explain how he was endangering his own life, he retorted, 'I haven't died yet, have I?'

He got himself barred from his best friend's house after he had managed to get hold of a paintball gun that one of the boys owned. He fired it at their next door neighbour's house, splattering paint everywhere. They had just had their house painted! The neighbours were justifiably furious and wanted to hit Stefan. They said they had already had dealings with him because earlier in the summer he had thrown a water bomb into the open window of the wife's car, which had been moving slowly over some road speed humps, and it had burst all over her.

Once or twice we allowed Stefan to go to a new disco that had recently opened for children aged between thirteen and sixteen. On certain days only, sixteen- to eighteen-year-olds were allowed in, and on one particular day Stefan and a friend managed to get in during this older session. Someone brought him home and he was in a bad way. I was told that he had had his drink spiked. He was very sick and ill and hallucinating. I was very worried about him and rang the hospital for advice. They told me to keep a close watch on him over the next twenty-four hours and to phone immediately if there was any significant change or deterioration in his condition. Fortunately he recovered within a day or so.

A few days later it was my oldest daughter's sixteenth birthday. Stefan organised a surprise party for her. He asked everyone at our church, and also relatives and friends. It seemed like he had asked the world and his wife as nearly fifty people turned up at our house! I decided to support him and not chastise him, as I felt that he must have thought about his sister and had bothered to try and organise something for her, which was quite touching.

A friend of Stefan's came to stay for a couple of days. I left them together at home for a short time while I popped to the shops. As I came down our road a little while later I noticed a police car outside our house and my heart dropped into my shoes. What now? There was never a dull moment at our house! Stefan had climbed onto our roof (again!) and apparently had been jumping from roof to roof across neighbouring houses. He had also been seen throwing a hatchet around the garden earlier, though goodness knows from where he had got it, and had been using very bad language with his friend. I banned them from seeing each other for a while. After the roof incident, Stefan was chatting a lot about a 'skylight'. Vaughan decided to get up on the roof himself and see if there had been any damage done. Our neighbour had been round and told him that Stefan had thrown a tile from our roof into his garden which had smashed a window of his shed, so he had phoned the police.

Sure enough, on checking, Stefan had done the unthinkable. Tiles were missing from the roof and a big hole was gaping right through into our attic. He had indeed made a 'skylight'! Vaughan was at the end of his tether. The next day the police phoned us about the incident and wanted to know if we intended to pay for the damage to the neighbour's shed. I assured him we would. Fortunately, he is the local officer who knows about Stefan and that he has ADHD, and was quite nice about it all.

The next night Stefan spat his bedtime tablet out. He was extremely lively and turbulent and by late evening he became aggressive and rude. He threw a whole large orange down the toilet. I made him fish it out so he flicked dirty loo water over me. I saw red. I had had enough this week. I tipped some water over him. He called me a b—ch. He did not settle until two o'clock in the morning. I felt worn out, worn down and utterly exhausted. What a week!

September

The police officer, who had by now come to know our family quite well, called in to check that Stefan was not annoying our neighbours. Sometimes, when he was on duty, he would just call by to see how we were doing. Fortunately, it was the beginning of a new school term and now Stefan would be starting a new tuition programme at a school some ten miles or so from home, where he would receive one-to-one tuition. A taxi would be picking him up and dropping him off at the school and returning him after an hour and a half. After his first day there, he arrived home as high as a kite and drove us all mad. But at least he was now getting some education, even if only for an hour each day.

During the middle part of this month, we had a family wedding to attend, and we bought Stefan his first suit. It had to be altered slightly, but he looked so smart in it: a really handsome young man. All our families were going to travel to France for the wedding, so it was going to be a grand affair. Unfortunately, just a week before, he got one of the neighbours (not the one whose shed window he had broken!) to shave his head and came back with just stubble in place of the lovely crop of blond hair that he has been blessed with. He looked like a convict!

I was always on tenterhooks whenever we went anywhere with Stefan, as I never knew what he would end up doing, and the wedding was no exception. A coach was hired to take everyone from England over to the venue in France and the journey went without mishap. However, during the reception, Vaughan was summoned to the main grand building to be confronted with a very irate manager. Stefan had somehow got into one of the rooms and onto the computer there and was looking up pornographic images. Grabbing Stefan almost by the scruff of his collar and apologising on behalf of his son, Vaughan bid a hasty retreat and reprimanded him.

The reception gardens were beautiful, with a lake surrounded by weeping willow trees. Stefan's next escapade was to throw himself fully clothed into the lake. He had to walk about soaking wet for the next few hours. A wine fountain had been set up among the plates of fabulous food. He helped himself to the free-flowing wine, unbeknown to us, and got very tight. I am so used to awful things happening when he is around that I guess I am no longer much surprised at many of the antics which the ordinary person would consider absolutely shocking. I think I would be more amazed if we ever had a trouble-free trip or outing anywhere!

Well, a few days after that wedding I ended up having a fight with my son. I was trying to reason with him about some matter when he became verbally abusive. I got angry and flew at him. The trouble is, he is now much bigger and stronger than me, and I came off worse. It was me who ended up crying my eyes out and nursing a bruised arm. I think he realised that he had gone too far when I locked myself in my bedroom and would not come out for some time. He got quite concerned. After this, the rest of the day went OK.

2000

His tuition programme seemed to be going really well, but as he was only away from home for about an hour or so in total, he got a bit bored during the remainder of each day. He was taken to various venues by taxi for his lessons, which he seemed to enjoy, but he was doing virtually no exercise. Instead he took to lying about at home watching videos. We still only allowed him to watch films which had a PG (parental guidance) or a '12' certificate, as he was particularly vulnerable and so easily influenced. Because he was getting bored at home, he began to have 'shops' on the front lawn again, and made himself £20 by selling some of his stuff. He informed me he was saving for a coloured laptop computer.

Just when I thought things might have been calming down for a bit, Stefan went round to a neighbour's house, lifted a pint of milk from their doorstep and drank half of it. The son caught him in the act and went mad. When it was brought to my attention, I made Stefan go to the shop and buy another pint with his own money and deliver it back to them, in order to try to teach him to take the consequences for his actions. However, the following day our friend the local policeman came knocking on our door. A garden chair had been taken from a lady's garden and the lady in question was certain it was Stefan. It was again a question of 'give a dog a bad name'...

I was most concerned about this latest event, but Vaughan went round to see the lady himself, and her story did not tally with what she had told the policeman. I had to take Stefan to the local police station to have a taped interview, and his fingerprints were taken, as some were found on a pot plant that had been standing on the chair and placed elsewhere in the garden at the time. Stefan hotly denied it. The policeman who knows him quite well by now was convinced that this was not a

'Stefan' sort of crime, and in the end he was dropped as a suspect.

I developed the mother of all headaches a few days later with an overwhelming tiredness and had to go and lie down, something I very seldom did. I would have to be feeling quite dreadful for this to happen and I really did feel terrible. Stefan was very concerned for me and was sweet and cleaned the whole of the upstairs for me (for money, of course). In fact he did a remarkably good job, even cleaning round the bathroom taps. Not to do anything without mishap, he rammed the lid of the spray polish into his mouth and it got stuck. I knew it was far too big for him to swallow and he looked so funny with his mouth wide open, lips encircling this lid, that I just could not help laughing, despite my headache. He tried to get it out but it was wedged fast. Even though I tried, I could not shift it, so he went off with his mouth gaping wide open around the lid, and played the piano. He looked hilarious playing tunes. It was stuck there for a good half-hour until finally he managed to squash the plastic really hard with his teeth and we extracted it.

Not much goes without some sort of disaster when he is around. Since the beginning of the month we have had to:

- Replace tiles on our roof.
- Replace next door's shed window.
- Replace our remote control after he broke it.
- Pay for damage to his friend's sunglasses.
- Replace both tyres on his new bike that he punctured.

Stefan is costly!

October

Stefan has three new obsessions on the go. The first is tennis! It is back on his agenda with a vengeance! He looks for people to play with him all the time. Anyone, anywhere, any time. His second obsession consists of phoning one particular lady from our church, for whom he has a particular leaning. She informed me that much as she loves him, she is getting fed up with his calls night and day. I explained this to him, that she must not be bothered by his calls all the time, but that she still loved him.

Vaughan took him to his snooker club one day. That was the trigger for the third obsession. In the garage, up went the snooker table that had been stored away. Stefan was outside there at every opportunity. At least they are all healthy and good 'obsessions'. Lately he has been better after school, and also with the one-to-one hourly education that he receives at the centres, although one can never predict what a day will bring forth with Stefan. One day I found that he had cut up one of my single bed sheets for his own use. He had also found one of my ancient long playing records (LP) and plunged it into hot water in order to try and bend it into a sort of bowl shape.

A national newspaper was running an article about ADHD, and a reporter arrived while the newspaper photographer was taking some shots of me as Stefan's mum. Stefan answered the door and told the reporter that the photographer was in the back room, 'Taking porn photos of my mum, because she is a prostitute'! I think he just likes the word!

The end of October marks the occasion of Halloween. As Christians, we do not hold with the tradition of 'trick or treat' and have explained to our children why we do not allow them to go knocking on doors like many other children do. However, Stefan had his own agenda, and despite not giving him licence to do so, he disappeared for a couple of hours on the two days over the weekend, returning with box-loads of sweets, crisps, biscuits and money. We were very upset with him for going against us.

November

We had a review of Stefan's tuition. He was given a good report and had made a lovely display cabinet in woodwork class. He showed it to the lady who conducted the review. She asked him what he was going to display in it. 'Mum's tampons!' he replied. He was very out of focus during the review and kept prodding the lady with a stick. He constantly lifted her hair, and kept touching her handbag and gabbled on and on about his snooker cues. It was useless trying to get him to concentrate. At least we knew that he was progressing with the tuition.

Vaughan took him to a boot sale to sell some of his constantly accumulating stuff. He made £50 and was chuffed to bits. He bought a mobile phone.

An ADHD support meeting was organised for this month, and I went along with Stefan and Vaughan, who came reluctantly. We sat with the other parents to talk and compare notes while Stefan ran off to socialise with the other kids, most of whom had ADHD too, of course. I was telling them how much easier it gets in many ways during the teen years, especially with regard to the hyperactivity diminishing, and I told them all how much better Stefan seemed.

Suddenly the pub manager came over to where we were all sitting and said that a boy in a check shirt was creating havoc. It took little guesswork to realise who it was! And there was I, boasting about how much better he was! Following the manager to the play area, we questioned the girls. Apparently Stefan and another boy had chased them into the girls' toilets and thrown wet toilet tissue over them. They had then smeared ice cream over the walls, and squirted Ribena under the toilet doors, where the girls in desperation had locked themselves in. Finally they had broken a toilet roll holder. I cannot remember the outcome, but I expect Vaughan would have made a hasty retreat with Stefan after a severe telling-off, and I would have been rather red-faced with embarrassment.

Dealing with constant bouts of Stefan's boredom and constant need for a 'buzz' poses a continual pressure to try and encourage him to engage in activities when the obsessions quickly wear off. He then watches endless television, moaning about how bored he is. I offer to take him to places of interest, but each offer is quickly declined. He says he wants his dad home. His relationship with Vaughan has improved no end lately. One night he was so bored that he had a bonfire *inside* the garage!

The new obsession soon emerged. He just *had* to get a Nintendo 64! He sold his mobile phone to his dad and scanned the local paper every day, phoning up all the numbers that advertised one for sale, and I ferried him around in the car so that he could examine the various ones until he eventually found the one he wanted and was delighted. Every time he gets an obsession he is literally transfixed with whatever it is and will constantly be playing or doing it until it finally exhausts itself and he moves on to the next thing. He stayed up until a quarter past two in the morning on the day he bought his Nintendo. He continued all the next day and the next, and the next, and the next… One evening Vaughan told him that he really had to go to bed and told him quite vehemently. Stefan was angered by Vaughan's tone of voice and answered back, 'You're a pathetic retard!' I don't know how Vaughan managed to restrain himself.

Sometimes Vaughan does a house clearance as part of his job. Stefan went with him on one particular occasion. He found a false leg which looked very realistic, and what is more it was flexible, so it could be bent about. It became his new obsession. He took it everywhere with him. He curved it around his neck, and played with it for hours. He finally he took it to bed with him. He usually takes everything that he is obsessed with at the time to bed with him, and once even took a bicycle up the stairs and into his bed to 'cuddle'. Oh well, maybe we know now what we can get him for his next birthday. False limbs!

Our monthly visit to Great Ormond Street Hospital was due just the week before Christmas. Stefan called the doctor 'an a—hole'. He drew on the table and chairs and fidgeted non-stop, begging to be allowed out of the room so he could go down the stairs. After we emerged, with me feeling a frazzled mess, we had arranged to meet up with some friends for lunch in London. Stefan was completely 'high' and almost out of control. He cannot cope with being with several people but is best on a one-to-one basis.

Sometimes after our visits to the hospital I would take him to Covent Garden, where he would enjoy watching the street entertainers, and thus was born a new idea in his mind after observing a bloke on a unicycle. He had to get one! So he did! Using his usual methods of wheeling and dealing, within a short space of time he had got the money together and purchased his very own unicycle. I had my doubts about his ability to master such a difficult piece of equipment but, not to be beaten, he was adeptly riding it within a day or so; not only riding it but performing all sorts of manoeuvres in mimicry of the street entertainers that so fascinated him.

Stefan quickly mastered the art of unicycling

Stefan's moods can switch from being very hyperactive to being very bolshie and objectionable, and he frequently does not relate properly in any conversation. I have noticed more recently that I can't get through to him or talk about anything much except about what he wants at the time, or his latest obsession, which at present is back to the Nintendo, which he plays on incessantly.

On Christmas Eve, the pedal came off Stefan's new suspension bike. I had to return it to the shop last thing just before the shop closed down for Christmas. The man in the shop remembered me. He looked at the bike and said it had been badly abused already. It was only three months old. Stefan was given some new mudguards for his bike on Christmas Day and Vaughan put them on for him. It took him three hours to do, as it was so fiddly. Stefan then decided that he did not like them and pulled them off, leaving a mess of screws, nuts and bolts all over the garage floor. To add to this, he went to see his friend and bought a different suspension for the bike from him, not bothering to find out if it would fit properly. He was well and truly messing up his new bike, and I was still paying it off! By the second day after Christmas, he had spent all the money he had been given – all £40! To make more money, he and his friend spent the rest of the Christmas holidays selling antiques and other items in and around our local area. As soon as he got any money, it would be gone immediately. He never seems to hold on to it for long. Goodness knows what he does with it…

2001

January

A neighbour who lives a couple of doors away came round. He is a very pleasant gentleman who is always ready to give a helping hand and with whom we often stop and have a chat. Would Stefan please stop throwing oranges and apples into his garden over the fences? He had also found some smashed eggs.

Stefan turned sixteen at the end of February. I can hardly believe it. He informed me that he could get married!

May

These are some of his antics that took place during this month. He sprayed our black dog with liquid gold. The poor long-suffering dog now hides when he hears Stefan come in. One time he put the poor creature inside a suitcase and slid the case down the stairs. If I had known about it at the time, it does not bear thinking about what I might have done. I was only told a long time afterwards – fortunately for Stefan. He threw a shoe very hard down the stairs, hitting Louise on the face because he was angry with her. He picked up a knife and lunged at her when she antagonised him. He threw eggs at passing cars. He had a bonfire in our wheelbarrow, using lighter fuel, in the middle of the night when we were all in bed, and left the garden in a complete mess. He broke into my bedroom, which I always kept locked, and took my powders and blushers and made himself a fake tan. Although he denied it, the evidence of red powder marks was left all over the dressing table.

He stole our family car one night and went on a joyride with the boy in the next road. He bunked his special school tuition one morning, telling the taxi driver to take him home. He was extremely verbally abusive to the husband of a local lady antiques dealer who had 'employed' him to help at her shop. He was instantly dismissed. He smokes!

June

Stefan has managed to get himself a little part-time job helping a local man to do some gardening and earning himself a bit of money. He wanted to buy a second-hand computer. But as soon as he earns a bit, he is out buying and selling all the time. He buys one thing, and then sees something he would rather have and sells the first thing to purchase the next. This pattern is repeated over and over. It reminds me of the fairy tale of 'Foolish Jack', who took the family's cow to the market to sell it, but traded it in for something that took his fancy, then something else and so on, and ended up with a few beans. When he arrived home his mother scolded him severely and told him what a foolish boy he was. Stefan is so like Jack. He has brought home an electric guitar, which he has then traded in for an old boat, which he has then traded in for a ring. The items, like those in the fairy tale, diminish more and more in value until he ends up with worthless goods. It is no good trying to point this out to him because he sincerely believes he has got himself a bargain each time.

July

Stefan made his first trip to see Vaughan's mum in Somerset with Vaughan and without the rest of us. He stayed a few days and peace reigned in our house. When he returned he had bought a rubber dinghy, which he was so proud of, and went straight off to the beach with some friends. He rowed out to the end of Southend Pier, which is the longest pier in the world. The lifeguards spotted him and were called out to rescue him. The current can be quite strong around the pier and I think that even Stefan was quite scared. Just after this incident, he told me that he and his friend had arranged to go waterskiing at seven thirty one morning. I was quite wary but I knew that his friend was a very keen sportsman and Stefan is a strong swimmer, so I helped him get his stuff ready with a change of clothes and even gave him a little bit of money. I kept urging him to go to bed as it was getting so late and I went off to get some sleep.

I was rudely awoken at two thirty in the morning by noises coming from downstairs, so I donned my housecoat and I crept wearily down the stairs – to be greeted by a couple of policemen in the front room. Stefan and the boy from around the corner had been reported pushing our car out of our driveway and down the road. They had intended to go off for a ride in the early hours before any of us were up!

Stefan had somehow and at some point in his life learned to drive, unofficially, of course. At breakfast time I rang the friend with whom he was supposed to be waterskiing to cancel the trip. The friend knew absolutely nothing about it. It was all a complete lie. I then rang the other boy's mother to tell her about the incident in the night. She knew nothing before I told her.

The police came back to our house during that afternoon and gave Stefan a grave talking-to about consequences of his actions and gave him a good ticking off. The boy's parents, with whom we were quite friendly, turned up in the evening with their wayward son and we sat the boys down and spoke to them both severely. After denying many times that they had intended taking our car actually out in order to drive it off around town, they finally admitted their wrong intentions and apologised and we all parted on good terms.

August

Stefan begged his older sister to help him dig up worms as he said he was bored. Long-suffering Jane obliged, and Stefan was happily collecting other creatures such as woodlice and beetles plus a slug or two. He cooked them in the frying pan, put them all in a sandwich and then *ate* them!

September/October

Stefan finished at the school where he was receiving one-to-one tuition and now that we were at the beginning of a new school year, he was starting a business studies course at the local college, with learning support in place. It was not long before the ADHD showed up. During the first few weeks, the students were taken on a trip to Alton Towers. Stefan rode on the monorail and threw his milkshake all over a man's head below. He crumbled up biscuits and threw them over the other students on the coach, and he smoked on the coach despite the prohibition. He was hard to control and his tutor rang me the next day to recount all of these incidences, telling me that Stefan had generally caused mayhem.

I had to go into the college for a discussion with the tutors about his lack of concentration and his calling out in class with inappropriate remarks and using bad language and being generally disruptive. I was told that one day he had unravelled reams of toilet roll all over the college, and another time he had filled a condom from the machine in the toilets with some Slush Puppy drink and thrown it down the college stairs. Targets were set for one month and extra learning support was drafted in.

November

Stefan put a live firework in the microwave. I just rescued it before it blew up. He then tried to make a 'bomb' by tipping gunpowder from two fireworks into some foil, wrapping it up and putting it in a tin to explode. He asked his dad where leather came from and Vaughan explained that it came from the skin (hide) of certain animals. The next thing we knew, he had made a wallet sandwich. For those undiscerning readers, this is how it is made, Stefan style. Butter two pieces of bread thickly with butter. Using some oil, fry one medium-sized leather wallet for several minutes. Place the wallet carefully between the buttered bread and attempt to eat. Later he told me that we should be able to eat leather as, after all, it is part of an animal, and we eat some animals!

I still have to be very vigilant and alert to what he gets up to. He still does not seem to realise that his actions bear consequences. Every single day there are new happenings. He stays up all night several times a week and I often find my eggs missing. He assures me that he eats them when he gets hungry in the night. I have checked the bins for eggshells but there are none. Maybe he is eating the shells too. I would not put it past him, but my guess is that he is still using them as ammunition.

December

Stefan went out in the early hours of the morning while everyone was still in bed asleep. There was no sign of him when it was time for college and I became very worried. At nine o'clock there was a call from the police station. He and another boy had been arrested at five o'clock in the morning. They were seen in a car supposedly trying to take stuff. I was extremely distressed and I also had to leave to go to my part-time job. Vaughan went to the police station at lunchtime for a police interview with Stefan. The matter was soon dismissed, as the boys explained that they had not been taking stuff but were merely sitting in a friend's car. We were most relieved. What worry he gives us!

One day during December, I had to go out for an hour and I left Stefan and Louise together. Louise rang me on my mobile shortly after I had left to inform me that Stefan was 'going mad' in the kitchen and throwing stuff about. I came back to find a huge wedge hacked out of our kitchen work surface. He denied he had done it. Shortly after, he decided to give himself a Mohican haircut in his bedroom. He shaved his entire head except for a plume on top. Using the food colouring from the kitchen, he had 'dyed' it blue...

In an attempt to channel some of his often misplaced energy we encouraged him to try and get himself another little part-time job to earn some pocket money, as the gardening job had come to an end. He made a few enquiries and soon landed himself some work between his college hours as a canvasser for a local double glazing company. He was very pleased with himself and very enthusiastic, although I had grave doubts it would last long before he tired of it. Sure enough, after just four weeks he was bored and quit. At least he did it for a month!

Just before the college term finished for the Christmas holidays, I received a phone call from them to say that Stefan had called one of the learning support team some very rude words. He was sent home and suspended for the next day and I was asked to attend a meeting to discuss things with the Head of Business Studies. It was like a rerun of his senior school before he had been finally suspended permanently. With a heavy heart, I set out to yet again plead his case, armed with information about ADHD. I explained how little he was able to organise, prioritise and socialise and how deficient he was in these skills. The Head of Business Studies said that she could understandably only make certain allowances, because it was unfair on the other students who wanted to learn, and told me how disruptive he was in class, calling out all the time, often very inappropriately.

Christmas that year was spent with my younger sister and her family in Cambridgeshire. The visit passed for once with relatively few mishaps. What a relief! But on New Year's Eve, Stefan went along to a football club party with our neighbour, who was reluctant to take him but was persuaded to let him accompany his own son. We found out later that he and another boy who had also gone there had smashed and vandalised the window of an empty office block that night.

2002

This is the year of Stefan's seventeenth birthday. In many ways it is quite scary. I have to increasingly let go of him as he is almost a man, yet it is quite worrying as he still acts so impulsively and hangs out with people often younger than himself, because he then feels he's the 'top dog', with them sort of looking up to him, and he is the one who will dare to try anything that only others think about but would never actually do. He also seems to lack a bottom line when it comes to limits of behaviour. This is very worrying. No matter how hard we have tried to instil values into him, he does not appear to have many. He went with our neighbour's boy to the house of a girl whom they knew to celebrate one of their birthdays. A week went by and I received a call from the girl's dad. He sounded angry. He had found a large new bottle of his liqueur had been opened and was half empty, and the other kids had said it was Stefan. Stefan told me that he had drunk a small glassful but that he had not opened it. The only way I could appease this irate father was to say I would replace the bottle, which I delivered shortly after.

The next incident involved another neighbour who lived a short distance from our house. Stefan and a mate broke into her house and took some priceless ornamental silver boxes along with the display case. I knew nothing about this until the other lad's father arrived on my doorstep to tell me that his son had confessed. At first I did not realise whose house it was but soon found out that it was a friend from our church. Shamefacedly, I went round to see her. She has known Stefan well since he was very little and also about his problems and she was incredibly nice about the incident and had not gone to the police, for which I was thankful. I promised her I would recover the goods and return them, but I discovered that the little blighter had sold two of the silver boxes to a chap at the snooker club for £15, and a gold one to an antiques dealer.

Vaughan was absolutely furious about it, said he could not stand any more and went off to Somerset for a couple of weeks to help his mother decorate, as he had no work booked in for his carpet and upholstery cleaning business. It troubles me greatly that Stefan appears to have less and less of a conscience. I just don't know what to do.

During one of our regular monthly visits to great Ormond Street Hospital, the specialist who saw him said that he is one of the most disinhibited boys he has ever dealt with. I am very frightened about how he will end up. It is all having a devastating effect on the family and the girls, as I spend so much time and energy dealing with a huge range of situations and incidents, and of course I frequently have to accompany Stefan to make amends with the various people with apologies, writing 'sorry' letters and making reparation wherever possible.

Well-meaning people tell us to chuck him out of the house, put him into boarding school, or other such drastic action, but I would never throw any of my children out of the house. However hard it gets I will never turn my back on him. No one can love a child like his own parents, and even though I feel driven to my limit so often, it is only the love I have for him, which is so strong and unconditional, that keeps me going; that, and my prayers for him daily. I have to believe that one day God in His mercy will turn Stefan's life around for the better, and I cling to that hope.

February

I got back from fetching my oldest daughter from Hatfield University to open the door to the police (again). A man and his wife had reported that they had been driving over the speed humps past our house when they had felt something hit their car, like a pellet. They had seen two boys hanging from a bedroom window. Their car had been slightly damaged. Stefan was nowhere to be seen. He and his friend Nick came in shortly afterwards and I questioned them both. They said they had not done anything wrong at all. They had been leaning from the window upstairs as Louise had rung the bell and they thought it was someone else. Later that evening, I found a number of my hard baking beans in Stefan's room on the floor, so it became fairly obvious.

Nick and Stefan have known each other most of their lives. One day they were recounting an incident that took place some years previously when I had taken them both to the park. They had nipped across the road to where my cousin and her husband lived, and had got into their back garden, where there was a swimming pool. My cousin and her family were away on holiday at the time. The naughty boys had filled the swimming pool with loads of thick logs that were always kept stacked by the changing room hut. They had then added the patio chairs. I never knew about this at the time. My poor cousin must have thought that some vandals had got in while they were away. Well, they had – my son!

About this time, I took Stefan up to London to meet up with one of the volunteers who worked at Great Ormond Street Hospital. He had got to know us a little when we had our monthly appointments. He was an elderly gentleman who took a great interest in all the children and was appointed by the hospital to direct people to the right departments and assist in many other ways. Stefan always looked out for him during our visits and did not like it if 'William' was not on duty the day we went. William had not seen Stefan for some time and he remarked on what a good-looking young man he had grown to be, and what a lovely boy he was. If only he knew some of the things that he got up to! I did not like to disillusion him too much!

I had to attend a meeting at the sixth form college, where Stefan was in the middle of the year's business studies course now, with the full-time learning support assistant. The Head of Business Studies needed to go through targets that had been set for him. We sat in the office, Stefan and I, while she gave a résumé of all the things he had *failed* at, from finishing assignments and handing them in on time to using abusive language to the teaching and support staff. She used the word 'failed' so many times that in the end I said quite emphatically to Stefan, in front of her, 'Stefan, you are not a failure.'

Not content with citing all the negative aspects, this woman concluded by saying that if he *failed* to comply with one more thing, he would be out, to which I replied that she was setting him up for 'failure', as she knew as well as I did that he would not be able to stick to it.

Sure enough, the following week, Stefan arrived home early from college saying that he had been sent home. I received a call from the college. Apparently he had brought up some inappropriate stuff on the Internet (ugly people.com!) and had referred to one of the pictures looking like a particular member of the support team whom he disliked. He had used quite abusive language to her after she had called him a little s—. He was suspended until an investigation had taken place, and I was to meet them at a referral panel. Vaughan was away in Somerset during this time and so I had to deal with this latest saga singlehanded. I found it all terribly upsetting, and in difficult times all I could do was to pray and ask for God's help and wisdom in dealing with each situation. I found it very difficult trying to cope alone, and more than a little challenging, as I knew I had to keep strong not only for Stefan's sake but for my two precious girls as well.

Prior to all this, I had booked a surprise trip for Stefan's seventeenth birthday. I had managed to secure two cheap flights to Venice with a booking at a youth hostel for a few days. I secretly packed a bag for him and myself. With passports and luggage hidden in the boot of the car, I got him to accompany me on 'a journey' on some pretext or other. Vaughan returned from Somerset, so he would be at home to look after the girls. When we arrived at the airport, I handed him the plane tickets with a 'Happy birthday!' and a big smile. The look on his face when he opened the envelope containing the tickets was one of incredulous amazement. 'Where's my suitcase?' he wanted to know. I told him it was all packed and ready. He could hardly believe it.

We spent a really happy few days together in Venice, exploring the canals, languishing in little cafés, visiting some of the main attractions, and even riding in a gondola (for a price!), and although it was much colder at that time of the year than I had anticipated, we still had a lovely time, just the two of us. The trip went without a hitch apart from the time he decided to eat five McDonald's in one day! I had not spent time completely alone with Stefan for a long, long time, and I hoped it would leave some lasting precious memories among all the other awful stuff that almost continually had to be dealt with.

Soon after we got back from Venice, Vaughan and I went to the West Country with the girls, to a wedding. Stefan had also been invited but chose not to come. I had received a tip-off that he was planning a wild party in our absence, so I had to make hurried arrangements and ask my sister and her husband to come to sleep at our house, which they kindly agreed to. But on the day we went, I received a call from my sister. Should she lend him £10 to go on the train to London? I said emphatically no, because he would borrow off people and never pay back. Also I felt unhappy about him going to London.

Stefan got on a train anyway and got caught for not paying, and the security guards had kept him at Liverpool Street Station. We were on our way back from the wedding when we received a phone call telling us that he had been taken to a police station, so we made a big detour from the M25 into London, where we eventually found the police station, only to be told that a mate had paid the fare and he had been released. I did not know where he had gone and felt quite frantic with worry, knowing that he is quite vulnerable and not too used to London, particularly late at night. We had no choice but to drive home. There was Stefan, sitting in the lounge, quite unaware of the worry he had caused! Also, while we were at the wedding, he had bought an old-fashioned pedal motor scooter from someone and had been riding it about. He had already crashed it into a parked car and caused damage, as he could not stop because the motor scooter had no brakes, and my sister had spent the day worrying about him.

On the day after our return, we got a visit from the owner of the scooter. Stefan owed him £60, at which point I gave up and told him he would have to sort it out with my son. I am fed up with people calling to the house saying that Stefan owes them money. It seems that every single day there is some incident or other, and it is not funny. I am so worried not only for his safety but for the wrong choices he is making. Then my phone bill arrived. He had run up huge costs. He had phoned mobiles and long distance calls, even to Greece and Australia. On one listing he had made seven calls in succession to the same mobile. He does not seem to have any sense of moderation.

March

Stefan got hold of a sharp kitchen knife and stabbed our downstairs toilet door over and over. The door was ruined. He broke his bedroom door in half.

We had to attend a meeting at the college with the referral panel about his future. There were five members of staff present, which made it rather daunting for both Stefan and me. I was handed a report of incidents to read – the story of our lives! I found myself once again in the position of defending his cause. They said he was unruly. They said he was difficult. They said all other manner of things, all of which were undoubtedly true. My response had to be carefully worded so as not to put their backs up or cause offence. I reminded them that the things that were reported were precisely the reason why he needed support; that he had special needs, which were part of his behaviour pattern, and that he did speak out of turn and out of context and display disinhibited behaviour; and although not condoning it, he needed to be given the same opportunities as the other students, albeit with unbiased support.

It was decided therefore that an application would be made for funding for him to receive ongoing one-to-one support so that he could finish the one year's course. A few days later the college informed me that they had been successful and Stefan was to start back the week before the Easter holidays for six hours a week with supported learning. I was to take and fetch him each time, to lessen the chances for any misdemeanours outside the college. This meant that the part-time job I had been working at over the preceding months would have to go in order for me to transport him at the given hours. The next few months resulted in Stefan gaining a distinction in business studies, which made the fighting for his place at the college so worthwhile. Oh, how proud we were of him!

Following this, we went to see the careers lady at the college, as Stefan had no idea at all about what he wanted to do next. He harboured a pipe dream about working on a beach in some remote foreign resort to earn a living, and could talk about little else. The patient careers lady talked us through the Prince's Trust programme, which was set up by the Prince of Wales to help young people develop their potential and learn to work as part of a team. It includes team-building projects, discipline and life skills, all of which Stefan needed. We even went to visit a unit to see more of what it involved, but Stefan was not interested, and no persuasion or encouragement worked. So by the end of May, when the college term ended, he had no job, no motivation and no incentive, and was spending most of the days sleeping and most of every night up and out clubbing till the early hours.

This pattern disturbed me because I knew that Stefan was vulnerable and could be subject to meeting up with undesirable company. Sure enough, no sooner had he begun this lifestyle than he was trekking up to London with a mate. One day he got himself into the company of a man who took an inordinate interest in him and his friend, unbeknown to me at the time. This man offered Stefan excitement in the form of taking him gliding. He gave him a mobile phone. He befriended Stefan big time. He even rang up one day and spoke to me, sounding most pleasant and affable. I was now alerted to his existence and the warning bells were sounding strongly.

Then one day something woke me up in the early hours. I didn't know what it was, but I went into Stefan's bedroom. He was about to leave the house, all packed up. I asked him where he was going. He told me that he was going to meet this man and his friend for a 'weekend away' with him, as this man had promised to take him gliding. I was horrified, and terribly concerned. I knew exactly what this man intended for Stefan but he seemed oblivious to the danger he was about to put himself in. By speedy intervention I managed to get hold of this man's number and rang and told him in no uncertain terms that my son would *not* be going away with him and that if he came anywhere near my son I would inform the police. A few days later, I rang the police to report what had nearly happened, only to be told that he was known to them and they were trying to find him anyway.

The next weeks were marked by a series of incidents with a

daily occurrence. Stefan dug up one of our dogs that had died some years ago and which Vaughan had buried about five feet under in our garden. He thought the bones would be 'useful' for research! Then he dyed one of our (living) dogs blue. My daughter invited a friend from school back to our house one day. Stefan tipped a bottle of stagnant urine all over her – it had probably been hidden at the back of the garden after one of his late night jaunts. Then one day I arrived home to find that he had taken a hammer to the garden shed. He had overheard Vaughan say it was time that old shed came down. He finished off the job the next day, leaving a pile of smashed wood where it had once stood. Another day I found a tin of white gloss paint in the bathroom. He had decided to paint his teeth!

No matter how hard I tried to change his pattern, Stefan continued to spend most of the nights awake, sleeping during the day. I tried to motivate him with ideas, or arrange things for him to do, but it was so difficult. Another time I booked for us to go to Norwich by coach to take part in a TV chat show, and Stefan took his friend with us. During the break time, the boys went around the town, where Stefan purchased a smoke bomb from an army shop and let it off in a bush near to where a lady was sitting, and nearly got himself arrested.

When I am out at my new part-time job, he apparently gets up to all sorts of mischief. He still takes delight in lobbing eggs, and he shaved both dogs with an electric razor, leaving a long shaven strip down each of their backs. Not content with one blue dog that he had dyed previously, he painted the other black dog gold, added a few touches of tangerine coloured paint to the other one, and bleached the tip of her tail white. I found the dog on top of his bunk bed unable to get down because it was too high for her to jump. I'm amazed the dogs still want to play with him!

Unfortunately, Stefan has started drinking beer. He smokes a lot more too, which I find distressing. I am learning to try and say as little as possible about these things, because the more I go on about them the more he seems to want to indulge. I just pray daily for him as I do for all my children. He brought home a jar of amyl nitrite poppers the other day. To be honest I did not know what they were. My daughters enlightened me. They 'disappeared' when he was not looking.

During his night vigils I found out that he was phoning people. That is, anyone randomly picked from the directory. At five in the morning one day he apparently called some lady and asked if she owned a cat. When she replied that she did, Stefan said that he was sorry but he had just seen it get run over along the main road. I was very angry to learn about this. I pointed out that this could result in some poor lady ending up with a heart attack or stroke through shock at hearing news like that, especially being woken up at an unearthly hour.

Another of his 'sick' jokes was to phone London numbers at about two o'clock in the morning advising poor unsuspecting people that there was a chemical attack over the city. He would say, 'Press one to speak to an operator,' and then he would disguise his voice, and carry on with a warning to shut all doors and windows and to stay inside their houses, as chemicals released over London by terrorists would cause severe illness if inhaled. My two daughters were alone in the house one day when they too received a 'call'. A voice on the end of the line asked if anyone had drunk any tap water recently. They were then told to go and run the cold tap and report to the caller what colour it was. There followed a warning that a dangerous chemical was in the water which had contaminated it and to go straight to the hospital, where staff had been put on full alert. My daughter had the gumption to phone the local hospital, and they had received no such information. It was fairly obvious who the caller was. I found it very worrying that Stefan had the capacity to think up such dreadful ideas like this. It more than bothered me. Why would he want to do such things? His dad and I gave him a very severe talking-to.

My birthday came round again. I went downstairs in the morning to find two huge jars of flowers. One contained bright yellow half-dead tulips, and the other a mixture of half-dead assorted flowers. Stefan had, as usual, been up most of the night. He told me that it had taken him about two hours to 'collect' my birthday present during the early hours. He had apparently picked one flower from each garden in the neighbourhood so that it would not be noticed, and he had 'borrowed' the tulip pot. How very thoughtful of the neighbours he is!

A day or so later I went out for a short while to walk the dogs, and as I was returning to the house I noticed smoke seeping through the guttering at one side of the house. Stefan's friend was up a ladder throwing water on to the guttering. Meanwhile two fire engines arrived with their sirens blaring and screeched to a halt outside. Stefan had dialled 999. Six firemen jumped out of the cabs and trooped into the house, while I stood in dumb amazement

Jane's door was always kept locked when she was out, and as the smoke was in that corner of the house, some of the firemen smashed down her door while others clambered into the loft. They thought that there was a fire brewing in the eaves of the house, but they found nothing at all and ascertained that the smoke was somehow connected to a barbecue that Stefan and his friend had started while I was out. After some period of time had passed, we figured out that he had probably sprayed some aerosol to create the effect.

What with events like this constantly going on, and my husband deciding to leave home, my older daughter in a depression at this point in her life and on the verge of giving up her college course, and my younger daughter being falsely accused of some misdeed at her high school, it is little wonder that I ended up on my sister's doorstep having a good old cry!

Meanwhile Stefan's antics continued. He had latched on to the idea of the hoax calls that he had been making and was enjoying this new pastime. He phoned the Automobile Association and informed the poor woman on the end of the line that he was 'Mr Patel'. In a most convincing Indian accent he told her that the car was stuck down a hole in Essex, and gave a name of a country village. He kept pretending he could not quite understand the questions, and the conversation continued with Stefan saying, 'Thirty metres? No, no, three inches... Yes, yes, front wheels down hole... Yes, I said *down* hole. No, no, can't get it up... Very, very dark... A torch...? No. I am not a member of the AA but I want to join. Money? No problem... I have thousands of pounds.'

The poor lady on the other end of the phone suggested he needed garage recovery, not the AA, but Stefan continued, insisting, 'No, I pay. Money no problem. I join AA. I give you credit card details.' This went on for fifteen minutes.

June

I arrived home from a cycle ride in early June to discover that Stefan had taken himself off to Brittany! He had gone without any warning. He had decided on impulse to go and visit a friend who was working on a holiday campsite in central France. He had never ventured this far from home by himself before. I received several calls from him en route. He was hopelessly lost. The railway in France was shut down because it was a French bank holiday.

It took him thirty hours to locate his friend. Then he was not allowed to stay on the camp, so he left and found himself stuck out in the middle of the French countryside at a tiny country airport. From there, he had thought he could catch a flight home, but only internal flights were available. The airport was so small it had shut down for the night and Stefan was entirely alone with no sign of life anywhere. He told me that it had been a really scary experience when he had felt the complete 'aloneness' of being lost in a different country with no one near and no family, no one to talk to and entirely by himself in the dark. He lay down under the stars that night with only the grass for a bed and the gentle lowing of the cattle in the nearby fields, and cried. And he hardly ever cries.

I had to put money into his account in order for him to get home. I managed to book a flight from this tiny airport the following day which took him to Paris, where I gave him instructions over the phone telling him where to go to get a connecting flight back to London. I was so utterly relieved to see him walk out of the arrivals at the airport when I drove to pick him up that I just gathered him in my arms and gave him a huge hug, fighting back tears of relief to see him safe and sound. I know that he so desperately wants to feel independent and he needs to as well for his own self-esteem, but I am also so aware that situations like this can arise, where I have to bail him out.

The day after he got back I filled up the fridge with the week's shopping, and stuck four family-sized pizzas in the freezer. To my horror, I discovered that Stefan had eaten three of them in one day. That is the trouble. He has no sense of moderation. He also took my car out and drove it around, but this time I caught him red-handed, as I returned home early from somewhere, and he did not think I would be back so soon. He has no licence, although a provisional one has been applied for. (I really must be mad!)

The police rang the house at midnight. Did I have a son called Stefan? I thought, They must have caught him, then, out in my car. But no, they were investigating an entirely different matter regarding an incident in a certain road that night. Apparently he had climbed the garden wall of a property with a mate and been for a dip in the swimming pool in their back garden during the night while the people were away, and the neighbours had heard the noise and called the police. The house in question was my cousin's (again)!

And so the antics continued throughout the summer months. Whenever I left the house for any period of time I was on tenterhooks as to what I would find on my return. Like the night I went to pick Jane up from the airport and left Stefan home alone, and he had cut holes in my tea towels. He continues to break things and he still throws eggs! I also warned him about associating with a certain boy in the neighbourhood, and that sooner or later trouble would occur. Sooner rather than later did come, when the boy in question arrived on our doorstep at ten o'clock one night. I watched him fiddle with the wing mirror of my car so I asked him to leave my car alone and please leave. He swore at me and said he was only returning Stefan's bike. He started shouting abuse, using filthy language, loud enough to wake the next door neighbour's children. There were several other youths with him, and also his mum and his girlfriend. He carried on and on shouting abuse all the way up the road, so the following day I rang a solicitor for advice, as I was feeling nervous about this boy. He told me that if he came round again I should call the police.

By the end of July, Stefan's provisional driving licence arrived, so I took him out properly in my car under my supervision. I was amazed at how well he drove, despite never having had a lesson in his life. I booked him for a course of lessons. I figured it would be better for him to learn to drive properly than continue to nick my car and drive it around illegally. After a number of lessons the instructor told me he thought that Stefan's lack of concentration might let him down, and Stefan himself was struggling, so he decided to give up the lessons. To this day he has never attempted to resume driving. In many ways I think that is a blessing!

Sometimes I have to give sanctions if Stefan continually disrespects certain things. I had to take his computer mouse away for a month when he refused to comply with a certain house rule. I felt terribly depressed all night because of having to keep the sanctions going. It really upsets me a lot and I feel absolutely horrible but I don't think I should just let certain things go. One of the main things about children or young people with an attention deficit disorder is that they do not learn from their mistakes. That is why I find it so difficult giving sanctions, because I know full well they do not work. I love him so much. He will probably never know how much, as I always seem to be telling him off and getting cross with him. But he is so impulsive. Last week he blew £130 on a tennis racket, which was just a whim. He is only on jobseeker's allowance, but as soon as his money arrives, he has to spend it.

This week he went and bought an £80 tent when we were in the camping shop. I nearly had a stand-up row with him in the middle of the shop, as he was all set to buy one for £100. There is no stopping him once he has decided on a course of impulsive action. To make matters worse, he then heard about a mobile phone with a £20 monthly contract going, so he was off to buy that the next day. Never mind about his phone debts, bank debts, or computer debts which are all well overdue – no, he must have instant gratification. It depresses me.

Jane's birthday came round again at the end of August, and we all went out for a meal in a local restaurant. Stefan gave her a slice of lemon and dared her to suck it! What he didn't tell her was that he had found it in the men's urinal and it was covered in urine – probably several times over by different visitors to the gentlemen's loo.

September

Stefan went up into the loft and got all the Christmas tree lights – several sets – and fixed them all over the underneath of his bunk bed. The dog has been painted again, this time orange. He takes great delight in feeding the dog with large spoonfuls of peanut butter, which he knows gunges up the poor dog's mouth.

It was a warm September evening and I had to drive to the freezer shop to collect some groceries. Stefan came in the car with me. He asked if he could 'borrow' a fiver to get a burger meal while I was in the shop. Shopping completed, I slumped into the driver's seat, exhausted. Stefan had sat himself in the back of the car and was acting in a cagey manner, maybe because he knew I did not allow eating messy foods in the car. I insisted he got out. He scuffled about a lot.

'If it's the burger hidden under your jacket, then you can eat it when you get home,' I chided, as he sidled into the front seat, still fiddling about under his jacket.

'Oh, what *is* the matter?' I asked. 'What have you got under there?'

I jumped as he suddenly pulled out a huge *rat*! 'What on earth…? Where…? How…?' I stuttered as the 'thing' attempted to crawl onto my lap. 'Get it off me please… *now*!' I almost choked while trying to restrain myself from opening the car door and taking flight fast. 'Is this what you call a hamburger? More like a rat burger!'

'I saw the pet shop as we parked up,' Stefan explained, 'and I really want a pet rat.'

'Well – *I don't*,' I said emphatically. I would have taken the darn thing back to the shop there and then, but they had already closed up as it was five thirty.

I was obliged to drive it home. I was cross that the shop had even allowed him to buy it without as much as a cage to put it in. 'Oh, I told them I had everything,' he said.

'Well, that was a lie! So where do you think you are going to put it?' I ventured.

'In my bedroom,' replied Stefan.

'Oh no you're not! You will have to put it in the garage for tonight,' I retorted, 'and then it will have to go back to the shop. There's no way I am sharing the house with a huge great rat like that!'

'It's cute!' murmured Stefan, stroking its horrid long creamy-coloured back. For the life of me I just could not fathom what was 'cute' about it.

Once home, Stefan proceeded to construct a makeshift cage in our garage with his computer table. I helped him tear up newspaper for the rat's nest and bunged in some cotton wool and water for it to drink. Stefan fed it with our best cheese out of the fridge, and eventually we retired to bed. I decided that the following day I would be returning it to the pet shop.

When I went to collect it the next day I discovered that during the night Stefan had sneaked it into his bedroom. I was also one hundred per cent convinced the rat had been cream in colour, but this one was bright orange! Had he bought two? On closer inspection, I realised that not content with spraying the dogs' coats, which he had done from time to time, he had now spray-painted this poor creature. Could I still return it? I decided to take the chance. I put it in a little box for the journey, and took it into the pet shop from where it had come, and spoke to the sales-person. I explained that my son had bought it the previous evening. They remembered him. I then went on to ask them if they usually sold pets without some sort of check on correct housing, food, bedding, etc. The sales assistant said that Stefan had assured them he had everything, so he had let him buy the rat. I told him the truth: that we had nothing at home, and could they have the creature back, please. They did not hesitate and took the box, tipping the rat into the cage with the other rats. The stark orange colour glared out but the assistant seemed oblivious to its overnight transformation, and even gave me my money back. I would love to know if anyone else ever bought that orange rat!

October

Stefan arrived home with a brand new laptop computer. He said he had won a competition with a service provider. He showed me the screen where it was written, 'Congratulations, Stefan, on winning a laptop with all accessories worth £2,000.' I congratulated him. A couple of days went by and then I found out that he had not won it at all but had bought it on credit at a local department store.

A few days later I was just thinking about turning in for bed when the phone rang. The police! Stefan had been caught shoplifting goods to the value of £7 in our local shopping area. I dashed down in the car. Louise wanted to know what was happening. I had to fob her off and I kept thinking as I was driving what a disgrace this was, and the repercussions it would have on the rest of the family if Stefan was dragged to court. The police were at the shop, along with one of Stefan's mates, who had been with him... but no sign of Stefan. The owner wanted to prosecute but the police advised him not to. I paid the £7 and tried to explain that my son has Attention Deficit Disorder and acts impulsively. The police wanted to see him at the police station the next day. I took Stefan's friend in my car and we went and found Stefan in the nearby snooker hall. He looked surprised to see me. He said that he had picked up some sandwiches and sweets in the shop with his mate and then walked on to the snooker hall, believing his friend was paying for them and his own purchases. But the mate had no money, so he'd told the owner he would go and fetch some and left his wallet on the counter as security. Meanwhile the owner had contacted the police.

The following day I had to cancel one of my own appointments to take Stefan down to the police station. Stefan spoke with a very nice officer who said that on this occasion no further action would be taken. He was given a warning. The officer said he understood about ADHD and that it was a nightmare to live with, as two of his relatives had it. Stefan was let off the hook.

One day in the middle of the month, Stefan walked downstairs with half of his head completely shaven again. The back was left all long. He had given himself a DIY haircut which had gone horribly wrong. Later, he called round one of his friends, who is almost as barmy, to finish off the job. The bathroom, Stefan, and his friend, were all covered in shaving foam mixed with hair – all down the mirrors, their clothes, the carpet, toilet seat and basin. Nothing seems to have changed much since he was tiny!

Towards the end of the month I arranged to have a rare evening out with a couple of friends with an Indian takeaway meal and a bottle of wine from the fridge that I had bought at the weekend for a treat. We served up the meal, opened the wine and poured it into the glasses. I took a sip. It tasted like water... It *was* water. Stefan had drunk the wine and carefully filled it with water, replacing the screw cap tightly. I was so angry that it almost ruined our meal.

2003

I have had to remove nearly all the medicines from the first aid cabinet in our bathroom. I found out that Stefan had taken most of them out and was busy sampling everything pertaining to coughs, colds, and flu, as he felt unwell. When he was younger we always had to keep the medicines carefully locked away for obvious reasons with a child, let alone one who sees no danger in anything. I tried explaining to him that it is not good to take combinations of flu remedies, paracetamol, and cough medicine. He said he wanted to dose himself up so that he could go out with his friend for the night.

I spent the whole of one afternoon sorting out Stefan's finances. He had been around town and visited two major stores and bought nearly £2,000 worth of computer stuff on credit. I managed to retrieve some unopened items to the value of £500. These I took back to one of the stores and spent ages on the phone trying to sort out the rest, including writing letters of explanation, and so on.

In November of this year we moved house. Vaughan had found the responsibilities of marriage, work, children and disruptive family life all too much to cope with and had left. It had been a very sad time, and quite traumatic for the children, but to this day we remain the best of friends and I shall always love him for the person he is and for the father of our three beautiful – now adult – children.

Stefan fought against the move – he hates change to his environment – and persisted in questioning why we could not remain in our lovely home. He did not seem to understand that I could not afford to stay there on my own with him and Louise (my older daughter had left home by now). He was, in fact, very instrumental in the finding of our present house, and very creative in his ideas about how I could make something of the rather run-down property that I had originally not given a second thought to. I reckon our old neighbours must have cheered when we moved from the neighbourhood and they could settle down to enjoy some peace and quiet, uninterrupted by the escapades of Mr Stefan!

I hoped and prayed that in this new house it could be a fresh start for us all, especially Stefan. I *so* did not want to cause any bad feeling with our new neighbours. Sadly, my hopes were very short-lived. The very first night we moved in, Stefan came home late and was sick in the neighbour's beautiful hanging flowering plant. I found out later that the owner is an avid gardener and submits his plants at flower shows. This was one such plant!

My neighbour knocked on my door first thing the next morning to inform me. My heart sank as low as it could as I profusely apologised. I suppose I had erroneously thought that things would be different in a new house, with a new beginning, where Stefan was not known. Of course, as with anything, we are who we are, and we take that with us wherever we may go. The characteristic behaviour of ADHD could not just be shaken off.

Within a few weeks of settling in, Stefan had explored his new surroundings and hooked up with a whole new set of 'friends', most of whom had problems of their own. Many a time I would return from work, or shopping, to find a house full of young people. I sometimes felt invaded, especially as without a male present, they did not seem to respect any boundaries I tried to instil. In addition, Stefan began to bring home large items that he had found dumped by people or thrown out as rubbish. I remember one day arriving home to find a huge grandfather clock sitting outside the front door. The fact it had no hands and a dilapidated clock face seemed inconsequential to him. Another time, I came home from work and walked into my front lounge to find the room had been 'taken over' by the most enormous television screen, which looked more like a home cinema! He had 'bought' it (on credit again) and had hired an extra large taxi to transport it home. The extra large taxi was called back, by me, and the huge screen promptly returned to the store, where I had to do the usual explaining about why I had to return it.

Old chairs would arrive home, along with other old

dilapidated pieces of furniture, including a very heavy exercise bench. This was displayed in my small garden, complete with old weights which Stefan threw about the garden, making large pit holes in my lawn. Most of the stuff had to be thrown out again, much to Stefan's annoyance.

Another time, Stefan broke down my bedroom door using sheer brute force when he wanted to get something that I had confiscated and was not even his. I have always kept my bedroom door locked, as it is really my only haven of privacy. You see, when he gets short of cash, which is nearly always, he will hunt around the house for absolutely anything that he can sell or pawn. I have come home to find video players gone, my DVD player pawned, even my CD player missing. I have nothing left in the house of any value. In some ways it has taught me not to place value on material things, even though it is extremely annoying and frustrating.

About this time, Stefan seemed to be getting a lot of sore throats. One day we were driving past the local hospital when he asked, 'Mum, can you just drop me off here, please?' I asked him why. 'I'm gonna pop in and get them to take my tonsils out,' he replied. He was being perfectly serious.

It made me chuckle. 'Stefan, you can't just pop in,' I explained. 'There's a little more to it than that.'

It transpired that some months later our GP did recommend that he should have those enlarged tonsils removed, and in due course the appointment came for him to attend the hospital. I drove him down in the car, we found the ward and he was booked in and given a hospital gown to wear, which he thought was an insult. They explained that he needed to be there during the afternoon before his operation and that he would be operated on first thing the following morning. Hating to have to wait at the best of times, he wanted to be seen to immediately and thought it was too boring to have to sit around in 'a silly old ward'. I stayed with him until visitors had to leave, assuring him I would be back the next day. I left him chatting and making friends with other people on the ward.

I was just settling down for the evening at home when there came a knock at the door. I opened it. There was Stefan, standing on the doorstep, complete in hospital gown! 'Hi, Mum!' He grinned. 'I got bored, so I decided to pop home. I'll go back in the morning.'

I was not only flabbergasted to see him, but also that he had walked all the way back dressed in that garb. 'You're going back right now!' I stated firmly, trying not to see the funny side of it all. 'You can't just walk out of hospital like that.'

'Well, I just did!' he replied.

I bundled him into the car once more and rushed him back. The ward sister greeted us, looking rather anxious. 'Am I glad to see you!' she said. 'Where on earth has he been? We've been looking everywhere for him. We even had a search party out looking for him around the hospital!' I told her what had happened. 'Now just you stay put, young man,' she softly chided with a twinkle in her eye. 'And stop giving us all shocks like that.'

The next day he was allowed to come home in the evening, after all went well with his operation. Inevitably, he had a very sore throat for several days and was given instructions to stay indoors for a week or so to avoid infection and to recuperate. Ha! Ha! Just let anyone try keeping him in! Within a day, he was off out, sore throat and all, despite warnings and pleadings to heed the advice he had been given. Not him. No chance!

It was a great achievement when Stefan secured himself a job working in a wholesale warehouse, where he learned to manage the tills, count stock and put it away, and help with van deliveries, among many other skills. Because he often stayed up most of the night, I had to make sure he got up each day, and it sometimes became quite a battle to get him off to work. Many a time I ended up driving him the eight miles when he missed the bus and then threatened not to go. It was during this time I wrote a few verses which I called…

Hurricane Stefan

A door slams open – 'It's gone eight!
Why didn't you wake me? Now I'm late!'
Belts into the bathroom – no time for a bath
He's grumpy and tired – keep out of his path.

'Do you want any breakfast?' 'No, haven't got time.
You know I'm supposed to be there by nine.
Can you lend me my fare? I'll pay you back,
And give me something to take – a quick snack.'
He whirls down the stairs and out the front door
Hurricane Stefan has struck once more!

I swallow a coffee – or maybe two –
And climb the stairs to the familiar view;
I can see even in the dark
That the 'hurricane' has left its mark.
I pull back the curtains – let some air in
Now the clean-up task must begin.

Drawers hang open, bed unmade
Clothes all creased and disarrayed;
A sock thrown here – a dirty one too –
Now where's the other? I haven't a clue!
Pants and more socks behind the bed,
Is it done on purpose to mess with my head?
I pick up clothes strewn over the floor
Whatever do I do this for?

Lying on the floor among the clutter
A half-eaten jar of peanut butter;
A plate – a mug – stuffed down the side
Some broken things he's tried to hide.
I hoovered the floor the day before –
You'd never guess, judging by the mess.

The day has passed all too fast,
And then a door slams – he's in!
Quick strides – a cheeky grin.
'Have a good day?' 'Yeah – can't stop –
Got to go up to the shop.'
'Want some dinner?' 'No, not now –
Not really hungry anyhow.'
I cover his plate and put it away;

Oh well, it'll do for another day.
The music starts and so I frown.
'We've got neighbours – turn it down!'

There's a knock on the door, a ring on the phone –
His mates seem to know as soon as he's home.
In and out they come and go;
From now on it's a constant flow.
And just as I am off to bed
Stefan gets into his head – to change his clothes
Then off he goes – where to? – No one knows.

Maybe to the park with his friends for a lark
They seem to have more fun in the dark.
And just as I am off to sleep
In the early hours back home he'll creep;
And finally his door shuts fast
And he will go to bed at last.
Until… a door slams open. 'It's gone eight!
Why didn't you wake me? Now I'm late!'

Whenever I went out, I always dreaded what I may come home to. I could not have peace of mind knowing the sort of things he got up to. But one New Year's Eve, we were all invited to my sister and brother-in-law's for the evening. Stefan was not keen to come and I was worried that he may try and invite people back to my house, so I read him the Riot Act, forbidding anyone to enter the house. To play safe, I locked several of the inside doors, including my bedroom as usual, the kitchen and the lounge. I also double-locked the front door. He assured me that he would be out himself, so off I went to my sister's with the rest of the family.

Just after we had all seen the New Year in, with lots of fun and a real family party, my sister received a phone call from Stefan. I needed to go home straight away. When I got there, supported by members of my family, the house had been trashed. A double-glazed window had been broken and my front door lock forced, two inner doors had been smashed, the wall scraped where the

TV had been forced against it, plants and ornaments broken, and my Christmas tree was not even there!

The drainpipe had been climbed up, according to my neighbours, and some 'mates' of Stefan had decided to party, knowing that I was out. A fight had ensued when Stefan had tried to get them all out, and then he had called the police. What a great start to the New Year! The next few hours were spent giving statements to the police, and on New Year's Day, a locksmith was temporarily boarding up the broken window to make the house safe. There was, in all, over £2,000 worth of damage done that night, and it took until June the following year to get it all sorted and repaired through the insurance.

We are now coming towards the conclusion of the year 2008. So it continues. There have been many, minor incidents with the police, and Stefan has spent many hours on a number of occasions down at the police station. They know him quite well now. Too many times to count, I have opened my front door to be greeted by the 'men in blue'. Stefan has managed to hold down one or two jobs, the one in the warehouse even lasting for over two years. However I later learned that he would often curl up on the top shelf in the corner of the warehouse where he worked, and have a little nap! He drinks too much and smokes too much, and almost on a daily basis there are situations to deal with, some of which have been quite serious. He still needs lots of support. He tried moving to the West Country with his friend for a short period to live more independently. Just before he announced his intention, I had written a poem:

> The piano thumps loudly, full pelt;
> The candles are on his TV and they melt.
> The fridge is rummaged, things disappear
> Instructions are given, but he doesn't hear.
>
> I walk right into a house full of boys
> They're messing about – oh! What a noise!
> My things aren't respected, the house is a mess
> And he stays out late – where? Anyone's guess.

> He loses his key, many times in a year;
> He does many things that others would fear.
> He grumbles at me, seldom gives me a hug –
> He suffers with the 'untidiness' bug.
>
> The cap's off the toothpaste, there's wee on the seat,
> The toilet's not flushed and towel not left neat;
> There's shaving foam over the taps and the sink –
> He speaks and acts before he will think.
>
> But when I am cleaning the mess from his floor
> And doing the same as the day before,
> I give thanks each day, though I may not show it
> More often than not, I go and blow it.
>
> And if I came back to a house all alone
> With no one constantly using the phone,
> And there was no boy here rushing about –
> A little light in my life would go out.

His dad and I took him down to the West Country and helped him and his friend find accommodation. We set him up with the basic things he would need, including a supply of food, household equipment and bedding, and stayed for a couple of days to help him get established. We left him there, then, and with rather heavy hearts, returned home. I felt it would only be a matter of perhaps a maximum of three months before he would be back. His dad visited him on a few occasions, as it was near to where his mother lived and so could combine the visits. On each occasion, he found that Stefan had completely run out of money. Although I was enjoying a spell of complete hassle-free living for the first time ever, I missed him too. It was strangely quiet without him. But it also gave me the time to focus more on my girls, and now some delightful little grandchildren.

Then one day in early February, I received a call from Vaughan. He was calling from Devon, where he had driven down from his mum's, and had found Stefan in a room all alone. The mate had left him and had returned to his home. Stefan was sitting on a bare mattress with no covers at all on a freezing cold winter's night. There was no electricity in the room. The window had a gaping hole in it. There was no food at all in the place and he had no money, and he was just in a flimsy T-shirt, freezing cold. He confessed that he could not cope any longer all alone and begged to come home.

They drove back through the night and arrived weary and forlorn. I had given him three months. It had been exactly that. I think the experience had been good for Stefan, but it had also made him realise that he needed support. Within days, things were back to how they had been before he left. Friends had heard he was back in town, and my house was invaded by a host of various youngsters coming and going at all hours of the day and night. The phone began to ring constantly, the washing piled up and food was consumed at a great rate. The men in blue started to call more regularly to question Stefan about this matter or that matter, and suddenly life was a whirl of activity, with all-night antics, untidy bedroom, loud music and general bedlam once more.

I go off to work each day never knowing what I will return to, just the way it always was. Although I make certain house rules, they are seldom adhered to. I may as well talk to the dog. We are now two adults living under the same roof. Stefan leads his life in his own different and bizarre way and I lead mine, and we try to jog along amicably, and sometimes we don't. I am there to support him as and when necessary, and at other times I just let him get on with things. He befriends the needy people who are around. He brings home all sorts of people and always wants me to take them in: people with problems, people who have dropped out of society and people who have difficulties. He has a very soft heart. He identifies with their problems. He wants to help them all. In his own way, he has taught me a lot. He is running to a different rhythm…

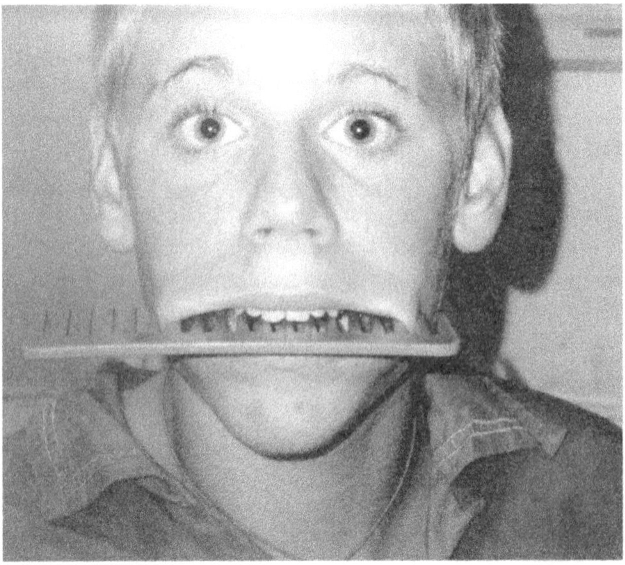

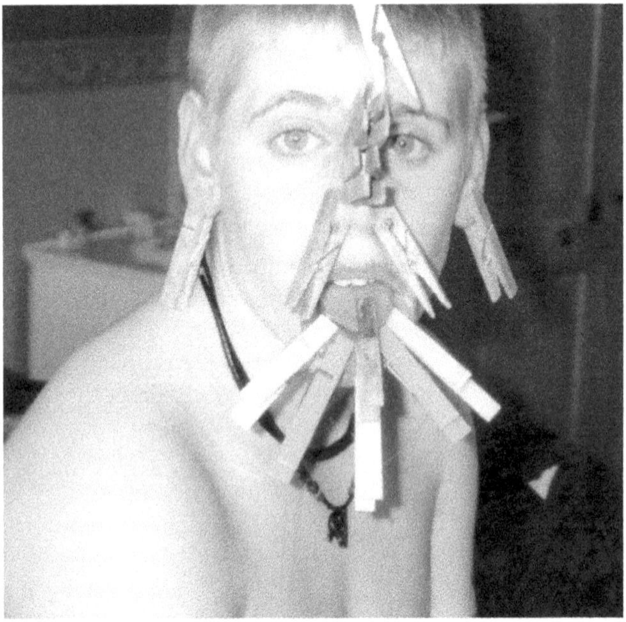

Afterword

On a positive note, people with ADHD are innovative, imaginative and inventive. They are not generally the run-of-the-mill, nine-to-five steady plodders of this world. They are people who seek thrills and excitement, who get bored more easily and who thrive on challenges and risk-taking to obtain the 'buzz' that they need to stimulate their impulses. If they learn to channel their enormous energy positively, they can become highly successful. They often become self-employed in business as they find it hard to conform to the demands placed upon them by employers. They prefer to call their own tune, using their own motivation.

All the values and standards we instilled into Stefan from early childhood are all there, deep inside him. I know it. He has a deep sense of justice and fairness. One day he will emerge all the stronger because he has had to cope with something different in his life and, by God's grace, he will find his niche. I love him for the person he is.

Research strongly suggests that ADHD and ADD are biochemical disorders in which neurotransmitters, the chemical messengers of the brain, do not work properly. It is important to recognise that the condition is not caused by bad parenting or poor parental management, but rather there is strong evidence that the cause is hereditary, being more prevalent in males than females on a ratio of one to four or five. Medication is usually prescribed, along with a behaviour management programme, although in recent years there has been some controversy surrounding the types of medication involved. New research is constantly being carried out to determine the best forms of treatment.

Symptoms Commonly Found in Adult ADHD

Some Negative Characteristics:

Impulsiveness

Difficulty following directions

Difficulty in setting priorities

Poor sustained attention

Shifting activities

Poor follow-through on plans, intentions

Easily distractible

Hypersensitivity

Poor time management

Procrastination

Temper/reactive

Losing things

Not listening

Short-term memory

Restlessness/fidgeting

Interrupting/speaking out of turn

Poor self-regulation

Poor social skills

High rate of self-medication, e.g. alcohol, smoking, drug abuse

Pessimistic, negative world view

Increased presentation of personality disorder (antisocial, passive, aggressive)

Low self-esteem

Some Positive Characteristics:

Creativity

Sensitive, empathic, deep feelings

Unique perspective, spontaneous

Fun-loving, humorous

Energetic

Leadership qualities

Usually highly intelligent

Winsome, charming personalities

Almost everyone displays many of the above characteristics at some point or other during his or her life, but for the person with Attention Deficit Disorder it is the norm, rather than the exception.

In 1990, Professor Berkley conducted an eight-year follow-up of ADD children and found that 80% were still hyperactive and 60% had developed either Oppositional Defiant Disorder or Conduct Disorder, which included some or all of the following:

Antisocial acts

Substance abuse

Underachievement at school/college

School expulsions/suspensions

Depression

Trouble with police/courts

More car accidents

Continuation of symptoms such as disorganisation, no self-regulation, inattentiveness and poor concentration

Pessimism – negative world view
Poor self-esteem
More unemployment
More geographical moves

Recommended Reading

Alexander-Roberts, Colleen, *The ADHD Parenting Handbook*, Taylor Publishing Company, Dallas, Texas, 1994

Hartman, Thom, *You Are Not Defective: A New Look at Attention Deficit Disorder Written Specifically for Adolescents*, Mythical Intelligence, Atlanta, GA, 1993

Richardson, Wendy, *The Link between A.D.D. & Addiction*, Piñon Press, PO Box 35007, Colorado Springs, CO 80935, 1997

Weiss, Dr Lynn, *Attention Deficit Disorder in Adults*, Taylor Publishing Company, Dallas, Texas, 1992

Lightning Source UK Ltd.
Milton Keynes UK
UKHW040623171118
332499UK00001B/6/P